The Bush

Universe

By Simon Burt

12 October – 12 November 2005

thebushtheatre

Cast

(In order of appearance)

Cock Dave	**Mikey North**
Mr Richmond	**Jeff Rawle**
Lauren	**Jessica Harris**

Director	**Sue Dunderdale**
Designer	**Bob Bailey**
Lighting Design	**Simon Mills**
Sound Design	**John Leonard**
Assistant Director	**Thorunn Sigthorsdottir**
Deputy Stage Manager	**Pia Jensen**
Assistant Stage Manager	**Lizzie Wigg**

Bottle Universe was commissioned by The Bush Theatre and received its world premiere at The Bush Theatre on 12 October 2005.

Mikey North Cock Dave

Mikey is a northern lad, whose training has involved work with the Stephen Joseph Theatre and the National Youth Theatre. His stage credits include *Spider Dance* (National Youth Theatre), Tom in *Old King Cole* (Fruitbat Theatre), Hansel in *Hansel and Gretel* (Dance Warehouse Productions), Don in *Singing In the Rain* (Dance Warehouse Productions), John Faust in *Faust and Furious* and Billy in *Billy Liar* (Pindar Players). He completed his first film role recently, playing teenage clubber Sam in *A Mind of Her Own*.

Jeff Rawle Mr Richmond

Theatre credits include *Way to Heaven*, *The Arbor*, *The Irish Soldier*, *Bent* (Royal Court), *Noises Off* (National Theatre), *Neville's Island*, *Queerfolk* (Nottingham Playhouse), *Releevo*, *Living With Your Enemies* (Soho Theatre), *Reluctant Heroes*, *The Elephant Man* (Churchill, Bromley), *Butley* (Fortune Theatre), *The Caretaker* (Thorndike Theatre), *Once a Catholic* (Wyndham's Theatre), *Equus* (Aldwych Theatre) and *Five Finger Exercise* (Upstream Theatre).

Television credits include *Sea of Souls*, *Spooks*, *A Touch of Frost*, *Holby City*, *Ultimate Force*, *Doc Martin*, *William and Mary*, *The Royal*, *The Deputy*, *Heartbeat*, *Death in Holy Orders*, *Take A Girl Like You*, *I Saw You*, *Fish*, *Microsoap*, *Neville's Island*, *Faith in the Future*, *Drop the Dead Donkey*, *Sharman*, *Blood and Peaches*, *Lords of Misrule*, *Look at the State We're in Chief*, *The Life and Times of Henry Pratt*, *Medics*, *Casualty*, *Minder*, *Rides*, *Moon and Sun*, *EastEnders*, *A Perfect Hero*, *The Gift*, *Vote for Them*, *South of the Border*, *Run for the Lifeboat*, *Boon*, *Fortunes of War*, *Call Me Mister*, *Remmington Steel*, *Country and Irish*, *Dr Who*, *Singles Weekend*, *Bergerac*, *Claire*, *Juliet Bravo*, *Singles*, *Wilde Alliance*, *Love on the Dole*, *Death of a Young Man*, *The Water Maiden* and *Billy Liar*.

Film credits include *Harry Potter and the Goblet of Fire*, *Blackball*, *Inspector Calls II*, *Baal*, *A Hitch in Time*, *Correction Please*, *Rating Notman*, *Duchamp*, *Crystal Gazing*, *Awayday*, *Laughterhouse* and *Doctors and the Devils*.

Jessica Harris Lauren

Theatre includes *Jane and the Magic Pumpkin* (Bridge Theatre).

Television includes *Fat Friends* (2 series), *Blue Blood*, *The Royal*, *Spoilt*, *Burn It*, *The Bill*, *Sparkhouse*, *Holby City*, *Peak Practice*, *Linda Green*, *Cold Feet*, *Heartbeat*, *How We Used To Live*, *Broker's Man, Finding Sarah* and *Smokescreen*.

Film includes *Ashes* and *Sand*.

Simon Burt Writer

Simon Burt was discovered by The Bush Theatre when he sent in his first play *Untouchable* in 2001, which was produced as part of the Naked Talent season, and was shortly followed by his second play *Got To Be Happy* (2003).

Simon's radio play *Another Big Day* was broadcast on Radio 4 in 2004.

Sue Dunderdale Director

Sue Dunderdale is a freelance director and writer, and is also the Head of the Directing Course at RADA. She has been Artistic Director of Pentabus Theatre Compant, the Soho Theatre and Greenwich Theatre. Her last production was *Cold Hands* by Chris Katic at Theatre 503 in May 2005, and her next production is *Mrs. Pat* by Pam Gems at York, Theatre Royal in February 2006.

Last year she wrote and directed her first short film, *Last Laugh*, starring Frances Barber and Doreen Mantle. It has played five festivals including Los Angeles and Chicago. She has directed numerous dramas for television and has two films in development.

This is her first production for The Bush.

Bob Bailey Designer

Bob graduated from Central St Martins in 1993.

Previous productions for The Bush Theatre are *The God Botherers*, *Stitching*, *Hijrah*.

Recent and current work includes *Falstaff* (Guidhall Opera), *The Real Thing* (Theatre Royal Bath and UK tour), *Macbeth* and *La Sonnambula* (Opera Holland Park), *Rent* and *Cabaret* (English Theatre Frankfurt), *Sweeney Todd*, *The Wizz*, *A Little Night Music* and *The Baker's Wife* (Royal Academy of Music), *Men* (Pleasance Theatre Edinburgh), *Love Me Tonight* (Hampstead Theatre), *The Lieutenant of Inishmore* (Theatre Royal Bath/Fiery Angel tour), *The Lying Kind* (Royal Court Theatre), *The Grapes of Wrath* (Finsbury Theatre), *Angels in America* and *Charley's Aunt* (Sheffield Theatre), *Translations* and *Moll Flanders* (Bristol Old Vic) and *Horseplay* and *Powergames* (Royal Ballet).

Other productions include *Tosca* (Nationale Reisopera, Holland), Jonzi D's *Aeroplane Man* (Theatre Royal Stratford East).

In 1999 Bob was the winner of the Time Out Designer of the Year Award for The *Happiest Days of My Life* (DV8 Dance Company International Tour).

Simon Mills Lighting Design

Current and recent work includes *Rigoletto* (Welsh National Opera), *Les Mamelles de Tiresias* and *L'Heure Espagnole* (Guildhall), *Tim Fountain.sex addict.com* (Royal Court, Schaubuhne, Berlin), *Nirvana* (Riverside), *Manon Lescaut* (Opera North and Norway), *Das Rheingold* and *Handmaid's Tale* (ENO), *Cunning Little Vixen* (Bregenz Festival 2003, San Francisco 2004, Geneva 2005), *Carmen* (Companions Opera, Gelsenkirchen Arena, Zurich, Shanghai), *Jenufa*, *Death in Venice* (Opera Zuid), *Julius Caesar* (Lyceum Theatre, Edinburgh), *Julius Caesar* (Young Vic), *Eugene Onegin* (Scottish Opera Go Round), *L'Elisir d'Amore* (WNO), *Cenerentola* (Opera Zuid and Frankfurt), *Don Giovanni* (Köln Opera), *Mattomeo 11* (Opera du Rhin, Strasbourg), *Paradise Moscow*, *L'Elisir d'Amore* and *The Bartered Bride* (Opera North), *Il Riturno d'Ulisse* (Munich, Copenhagen 2005 and WNO 2006), *Vixen Sharp Ears* and *Two Widows* (City of Birmingham Touring Opera) and *The Heiress* (National Theatre).

John Leonard Sound Design

John started work in theatre sound over 30 years ago and during that time he has provided soundtracks for theatres all over the world. He is the author of a widely-praised book on Theatre Sound, now in preparation for its second edition, and has been the recipient of a Drama Desk award, Sound Designer of The Year award and an honorary Fellowship of The Guildhall School Of Music and Drama.

Recent productions include: *Les Liaisons Dangereuses*, *Sweet Panic*, *Absolutely! (perhaps)*, *The Old Masters*, *The Birthday Party*, *The Anniversary*, *Hedda Gabler*, *The Master Builder*, *Losing Louis* (West End); *Jumpers*, (National Theatre, West End and Broadway); *The U.N. Inspector*, *Paul* (National Theatre); *Private Lives* (West End and Broadway), *Midnight's Children* (London, New York and UK Tour), *Antony and Cleopatra*, *Much Ado About Nothing*, *The Prisoner's Dilemma* (RSC); *Twelfth Night*, *The Merchant of Venice*, *The Merry Wives Of Windsor*, *Cymbeline* (Ludlow Festival); *Sunday Father*, *Osama The Hero*, *A Single Act* (Hampstead); *Five Gold Rings*, *The Mercy Seat*, *I.D.*, *Macbeth*, *Brighton Rock* (Almeida); *Guantanamo* (Tricycle Theatre & West-End); *Under Milk Wood* (Wales Theatre Company & National Tour); *Flush*, *Mercy*, *Colder Than Here* (Soho Theatre Co); *The Entertainer*, *Still Life and The Astonished Heart*, *Ma Rainey's Black Bottom*, *The Odd Couple*, *Who's Afraid Of Virginia Woolf?* (Liverpool Playhouse) and *Madame Tussaud's Exhibition* (New York, Warwick Castle, Amsterdam and Shanghai).

Thorunn Sigthorsdottir Assistant Director

Thorunn trained at the Flanders opera studio in Belgium, the Musikhochschule in Trossingen, Germany and the Reykjavík Music Academy.

Directing work includes *The Eighties* (Kópavogur, Iceland), *Devil's Island* (Ísafjördur Upper Secondary School, West Iceland), *Happy End* (Reykjavík Summer Opera), *Quarter* (Idnó Theatre, Reykjavík) and *Luisa Miller* (Antwerp Opera House).

Opera credits include *Diana* (Belgium), *Im Schatten Tallard* (Bär, Germany) and abridged versions of *Cosí fan tutte*, *The Marriage of Figaro*, *La Bohéme*, *Ballo Mascera*. She has also performed in various concerts and recitals in Germany, Iceland, The Netherlands and Belgium.

At The Bush Theatre

Artistic Director	**Mike Bradwell**
Executive Producer	**Fiona Clark**
Finance Manager	**David Smith**
Literary Manager	**Abigail Gonda**
Marketing Manager	**Nicki Marsh**
Production Manager	**Robert Holmes**
Theatre Administrator	**Nic Wass**
Technical Manager	**Matt Kirby**
Resident Stage Manager	**Ros Terry**
Literary Assistant	**Holly Hughes**
Administrative Assistant	**Lydia Fraser-Ward**
Box Office Supervisor	**Dominique Gerrard**
Box Office Assistants	**Ruth O'Dowd**
	Amanda Wright
Front of House Duty	**Kellie Batchelor**
Managers	**Adrian Christopher**
	Lois Tucker
	Catherine Nix-Collins
	Sarah O'Neill
Associate Artists	**Tanya Burns**
	Es Devlin
	Paul Miller
Press Representation	**Alexandra Gammie**
	020 7837 8333
Marketing Consultant	**Paul Savident**
	020 8567 2089
Graphic Design	**Stem Design**
	admin@stemdesign.co.uk
Sheila Lemon Writer in Residence	**Jennifer Farmer**
Pearson Writer in Residence	**Steve Thompson**

The Bush Theatre continues to develop its Writers Development Programme with the generous support of the Peggy Ramsay Foundation Award 2002.

The Bush Theatre
Shepherds Bush Green
London W12 8QD

The Alternative Theatre Company Ltd. (The Bush Theatre) is a
Registered Charity number: 270080.
Co. registration number 1221968. VAT no. 228 3168 73.

The Bush Theatre

The Bush Theatre opened in April 1972 in the upstairs dining room of The Bush Hotel, Shepherds Bush Green. The room had previously served as Lionel Blair's dance studio. Since then, The Bush has become the country's leading new writing venue with over 350 productions, premiering the finest new writing talent.

"One of the most vibrant theatres in Britain, and a consistent hotbed of new writing talent." Midweek magazine

Playwrights whose works have been performed here at The Bush include:

Stephen Poliakoff, Robert Holman, Tina Brown, Snoo Wilson, John Byrne, Ron Hutchinson, Terry Johnson, Beth Henley, Kevin Elyot, Doug Lucie, Dusty Hughes, Sharman Macdonald, Billy Roche, Tony Kushner, Catherine Johnson, Philip Ridley, Richard Cameron, Jonathan Harvey, Richard Zajdlic, Naomi Wallace, David Eldridge, Conor McPherson, Joe Penhall, Helen Blakeman, Lucy Gannon, Mark O'Rowe and Charlotte Jones.

The theatre has also attracted major acting and directing talents including Bob Hoskins, Alan Rickman, Antony Sher, Stephen Rea, Frances Barber, Lindsay Duncan, Brian Cox, Kate Beckinsale, Patricia Hodge, Simon Callow, Alison Steadman, Jim Broadbent, Tim Roth, Jane Horrocks, Gwen Taylor, Mike Leigh, Mike Figgis, Mike Newell and Richard Wilson.

Victoria Wood and Julie Walters first worked together at The Bush, and Victoria wrote her first sketch on an old typewriter she found backstage.

In over 30 years, The Bush has won over one hundred awards and recently received The Peggy Ramsay Foundation Project Award 2002. Bush plays, including most recently *The Glee Club*, have transferred to the West End. Off-Broadway transfers include *Howie the Rookie* and *Resident Alien*. Film adaptations include *Beautiful Thing* and *Disco Pigs*. Bush productions have toured throughout Britain, Europe and North America, most recently *Stitching*. In March 2004 *Adrenalin... Heart* represented the UK in the Tokyo International Arts Festival.

Every year we receive over fifteen hundred scripts through the post, and we read them all. According to The Sunday Times:

"What happens at The Bush today is at the very heart of tomorrow's theatre"

That's why we read all the scripts we receive and will continue to do so.

Mike Bradwell
Artistic Director

Fiona Clark
Executive Producer

Be There At The Beginning

The Bush Theatre is a writer's theatre – dedicated to commissioning, developing and producing exclusively new plays. Up to seven writers each year are commissioned and we offer a bespoke programme of workshops and one-to-one dramaturgy to develop their plays. Our international reputation of over thirty years is built on consistently producing the very best work to the very highest standard.

With your help this work can continue to flourish.

The Bush Theatre's Patron Scheme delivers an exciting range of opportunities for individual and corporate giving, offering a closer relationship with the theatre and a wide range of benefits from ticket offers to special events. Above all, it is an ideal way to acknowledge your support for one of the world's greatest new writing theatres.

To join, please pick up an information pack from the foyer, call 020 7602 3703 or email info@bushtheatre.co.uk

We would like to thank our current members and invite you to join them!

Rookies
Anonymous
Ross Anderson
Casarotto Ramsay
  Associates Ltd.
Geraldine Caulfield
Nina Drucker
John Gowers
Sian Hansen
Lucy Heller
Mr G Hopkinson
Ray Miles
Malcolm & Liliane Ogden
Clare Rich &
  Robert Marshall
Tracey Scoffield
Martin Shenfield
Alison Winter

Beautiful Things
Anonymous
Alan Brodie
Kate Brooke
David Brooks
Clive Butler
Jeremy Conway
Clyde Cooper
Patrick & Anne Foster
Vivien Goodwin
Sheila Hancock
William Keeling
Laurie Marsh
Michael McCoy
Mr & Mrs A Radcliffe
John Reynolds
Mr and Mrs
  George Robinson
Barry Serjent
John & Tita Shakeshaft
Brian D Smith
Barrie & Roxanne Wilson

Glee Club
Anonymous
Jim Broadbent
Nick Marston
Alan Rickman

Handful of Stars
Gianni Alen-Buckley

Lone Star
Princess of Darkness

Bronze Corporate Membership
Anonymous
Act Productions Ltd

Silver Corporate Membership
Anonymous
The Agency (London) Ltd
Oberon Books Ltd

Platinum Corporate Membership
Anonymous

The Bush writers: 1972 - 2005

The Bush writers are listed in alphabetical order followed by their Bush-produced plays.

* denotes where the title is available from The Bush bookshop.

The Bush Book, edited by Mike Bradwell and packed with anecdotes, is an essential guide to the first 25 years of new writing at The Bush. The Bush Book is published by Methuen and priced at £9.99.

Adam, Henry
*Among Unbroken Hearts** (2001)

Adamson, Samuel
*Drink, Dance, Laugh and Lie** (1999), *Clocks and Whistles*, winner of Time Out award and Pearson TV writers residency (1996), *Alice's Diner* (1990)

Adshead, Kay
*Bites** (2005), *The Bogus Woman**, winner of Fringe First award (2001)

Almaz, Michael
The Moshe Dayan Extravaganza (1974), *Monsieur Artaud* (1972)

Anderson, Sara Pia
Last Resort (1979), *First Blush* (1978), *Blisters* with Sheila Kelly (1977), *Gin Trap* with Sheila Aelly (1976),

Arden, John
The Ballygombeen Bequest with Margaretta D'Arcy (1972)

Ashton, David
*Buried Treasure**, finalist in LWT plays on stage award (1996), *The Chinese Wolf** (1993), *A Bright Light Shining** (1991)

Bandele-Thomas, Biyi
Two Horsemen (1994)

Barker, Howard
Wax (1976), *Skipper & My Sister and I* (1973)

Barlow, Patrick
*The Messiah** with additional material by John Ramm, Julian Hough and Jude Kelly (2000), *Love Upon the Throne** (1998)

Barnes, Brian D
Pickwick's Christmas Party (1972)

Barry, Sebastian
White Woman Street (1992)

Bauer, Wolfgang
Magic Afternoon (1976)

Bean, Richard
*The God Botherers** (2003)

Bennett, Colin
Soon (1976)

Bent, Simon
Sugar Sugar (1998), *Goldhawk Road**, winner of Time Out award (1996), *Bad Company* (1994)

Bentley, Eric
Are You Now, Or Have You Ever Been (1977)

Bicat, Tony
*A Buyer's Market** (2002), *Zigomania* (1978)

Blakeman, Helen
*Normal**, winner of the Pearson award for best play (2000), *Caravan*, winner of the George Devine award for most promising play and the Pearson TV writers residency award (1997)

Block, Simon
*A Place at the Table** (2000)

Bolstad, Mette
*One Life and Counting** (1999)

Bond, Edward
Jackets II (1990), *The Pope's Wedding* (1973)

Bradwell, Mike
China (1986), *Still Crazy After All These Years* (1981), *Ooh La La!* (1980), *A Bed of Roses* (1978), *Bridget's House* (1976), *Oh What!* (1975), *Granny Calls the Tune* (1975), *The Knowledge* (1974)

Brogger, Erik
Copperhead (1985), *The Paranormal Revue* (1979)

Broughton, Patrick
Forgotten Dreams and *End of the Road* (1972)

Brown, Ian
Runners (1978)

Brown, Tina
Happy Yellow (1977), *Under the Bamboo Tree* (1973)

Bruce, Lesley
*Keyboard Skills** (1993)

Bullmore, Amelia
*Mammals** (2005)

Burrows John
It's a Girl (1987), *Loud Reports* with John Harding and Peter Skellern (1975)

Burt, Simon
*Untouchable** (2002), *Got To Be Happy** (2003)

Buznea, Magdalena
For the Love of Piaf (1972)

Byrne, John
Candy Kisses (1984), *Writer's Cramp* (1977)

Cameron, Richard
*Gong Donkeys** (2004), *The Glee Club* (2002 & 2004), *All of you Mine** (1997), *The Mortal Ash** (1994), *Not Fade Away* (1993), *Pond Life* (1992)

Campbell, Ken
Psychosis Unclassified (1977)

Captain, Phantom
Abracadabra Honeymoon (1980), *Open to Question* (1976)

Cartwright, Jim
Kiss the Sky (1996)

Carville, Daragh
Language Roulette, winner of Stewart Parker award and Meyer-Whitworth award (1997)

Chapman, John
Marbles with Tim Fywell & Nigel Williams (1974)

Coghlan, Lin
*Kingfisher Blue** (2005)

Coles, Helen
*Crossing the Equator** (1995), *Backstroke in a Crowded Pool**, winner of the Susan Smith Blackburn prize (1993)

Copley, Paul
Tapster (1981), *Viaduct* (1980), *Pillion* (1977)

Coxon, Lucinda
Wishbones (1997), *Waiting at the Water's Edge* (1993)

Coyne, Kevin
England, England with Snoo Wilson (1977)

Crane, Richard
Decent Things (1975), *Secrets* (1974)

Cresswell, Jane
The One Sided Wall with Niki Johnson (1989)

Crompton, Michael
The Kiss of Life (1991)

Cullen, Mike
The Cut (1994)

Darke, Nick
The Oven Glove Murders (1986)

Davis, Stephen
Love Field (1987), *A View of Kabul* (1982), *The Last Elephant* (1981)

Dawson, James
Scene (1974)

Dowie, John
Only Men Shave (1978), *The Naked Obsessions of ...* (1976)

Drain, Richard
Hudson's Amazing Money Making Steam Driven Railway (1973), *Life in a Chocolate Factory* (1973), *Limbo* (1973)

Drury, Alan
Asides (1974)

Edgar, David
Blood Sports (1976), *Dick Deterred* (1974), *Operation Iskra* (1974), *Tedderella* (1973)

Edmett, Nicholas
Felons with Joe Griffiths (1976)

Edmundson, Helen
The Clearing*, winner of the John Whiting award and Time Out best play award (1993)

Eldridge, David
M.A.D.* (2004), *Serving it up**, winner of Time Out award (1996)

Elyot, Kevin
Coming Clean, winner of the Samuel Beckett award (1982)

English, Rose
The Beloved (1985)

Evaristi, Marcella
Breach of the Peace (1982)

Eyen, Tom
The White Hore and *The Bit Player* (1972)

Falla, Jonathan
Topokana Martyr's Day, winner of the Plays and Players award (1983)

Fannin, Hilary
Mackerel Sky (1997)

Farr, David
The Danny Crowe Show* (2001)

Fitch, Georgia
adrenalin...heart (2002 & 2004)

Fletcher, Paddy
Strut and Fret (1972)

Fountain, Tim
Resident Alien* (1999)

Frost, Emma
Airsick* (2003)

Fuhmann, Franz
The Fallen Angel (1991)

Gale, David
The Sleeping Quarters of Sofia (1975), *White Men Dancing* (1975), *Jack ... the Flames* (1974)

Gannon, Lucy
Dancing Attendance (1990), *Raping the Gold*, winner of the Plays and Players award for most promising playwright and the Arts Council residency award (1988)

Garner, Julian
Golden Leaf Strut (1981)

Gems, Jonathan
The Tax Exile, winner of the George Devine award (1979)

Gibbs, Peter
Rumblings (1985)

Gibson, Harry
Filth (2000), *Trainspotting* (1995)

Greer, Terence
Nobody Knew They Were There (1975)

Griffiths, Trevor
Who Shall be Happy ...? (1996)

Hall, Jonathan
Flamingos (2001)

Hannan, Chris
The Baby (1993), *The Evil Doers*, winner of the Time Out best play award and Charrington London fringe award for best play (1990)

Hardin, Hershel
Esker Mike and his wife Agiluk (1973)

Harding, John
For Sylvia with John Burrows (1972)

Harding, Michael
Misogynist (1992)

Harrison, Frederick
Subjects for Interrogation (1979)

Harrower, David
Knives in Hens (1995)

Harvey, Jonathan
Beautiful Thing, winner of Thames TV writers residency award, John Whiting award, Evening Standard award for most promising playwright and London fringe award for best production (1993), *Boom Bang-a-bang** (1995)

Haygarth, Tony
The Hard Stool (1976)

Henley, Beth
Crimes of the Heart (1983), *The Miss Firecracker Contest* (1982)

Herlihy, James Leo
Terrible Jim Fitch and Laughs etc (1972)

Hitchmough, Jim
Watching (1986)

Holborough, Jacqueline
Dreams of San Francisco, winner of the Thames TV award (1987), *The Garden Girls*, winner of the Thames TV award and the Time Out best play award (1986), *The Way South* (1989)

Holman, Robert
Making Noise Quietly (1986), *The Estuary* (1980), *Outside the Whale* (1978), *German Skerries*, winner of the George Devine award (1977)

Hornick, Neil
Kingdom Come, the Art and Craft of Pornography (1972)

Hughes, Declan
Digging for Fire, winner of the Time Out award for best play (1992), *New Morning* (1993)

Hughes, Dusty
Commitments, drama award for most promising playwright (1980), *In at the Death* (1978)

Hutchinson, Caroline
Heart Throb (1988)

Hutchinson, Ron
Eejits (1978)

Ikoli, Tunde
On the Out (1978)

Innaurato, Albert
The Transfiguration of Benno Blimpie (1978)

James, Terence
Story Tellers (1974)

Jarry, Alfred
Supermale (1974)

Jenkin, Leonard
Kitty Hawk (1975)

Johnson, Catherine
Little Baby Nothing* (2003), *Shang-a-Lang* (1998), *Dead Sheep*, winner of Thames TV award for best play and best production (1991), *Boys Mean Business*, winner of the Thames TV award (1989)

Johnson, Terry
Unsuitable for Adults (1984), *Amabel* (1979)

Johnston, Alex
Deep Space (1998)

Johnstone, Keith
Moby Dick (1975)

Jones, Charlotte
In Flame (1999)

Jourdheuil, Jean
Melancholy Jacques (1984)

Kearsey, Julia
Wednesday (1979)

Kemp, Lindsay
Flowers (1974), *The Turquoise Pantomime* (1973)

Kempinski, Tom
Duet for One, winner of 27 drama awards including best new play (1980)

Kennelly, Brendan
Cromwell (1991)

Kops, Bernard
More Out Than In (1980)

Kotak, Ash
*Hijra** (2000)

Krichefski, Bernard
A Perfect Retreat (1981)

Kroetz, Franz Xaver
Request Programme (1986), *The Nest*
(1986), *Through the Leaves* (1985),
Geisterbahn (1976), *Stallerhof* (1974)

Kushner, Tony
A Bright Room Called Day (1988)

Langham, Chris
Ggreasy Spoon with Richard Fagen
(1974), *Retrogrim's Progress* (1974)

Lavery, Bryony
*Goliath** (1997)

Lawrence, Maureen
Resurrection (1996)

Lee, Mark
California Dog Fight (1985)

Leigh, Mike
The Silent Majority (1974)

Lemkow, Tutte
Once Upon a Fiddle (1974), *Report to
the Academy* (1974)

Letts, Tracy
Killer Joe, winner of the Time Out award
(1995)

Lucie, Doug
*The Green Man** (2003), *Love You Too**
(1998), *Hard Feelings* (1983), *Progress**
(1984)

Macdonald, Claire
Utopia (1989), *An Imitation of Life* with
Pete Brooks (1987)

Macdonald, Sharman
The Brave (1988), *When I was a Girl I
used to Scream and Shout*, winner of the
Evening Standard most promising
playwright award and the Thames TV
award (1984)

Macgregor, Roy
Phoenix (1992), *Our Own Kind*, winner of
Meyer-Whitworth award (1991)

Mamaine, Arthur
The Prosecution (1972)

Mandvi, Asif
Sakina's Restaurant (2001)

Marcus, Frank
Christmas Carol (1972)

Marshall, Jonathan
A Wet Winter Night's Dream (1973), How
to Survive in the Nick (1973), *There's
Always Room in the Nick* (1973)

Materic, Mladen
Tattoo Theatre (1987)

Mathias, Sean
A Prayer for Wings (1985)

Matura, Mustapha
Independence (1979)

McClure, James
Lone Star and *Private Wars* (1980)

McGrath, John
*Plugged In (*1972)

McGrath, Michael
Third Flight (1980)

McLeod, Jenny
*Raising Fires**, winner of LWT plays on
stage award (1994)

McPherson, Conor
*St Nicholas** (1997), *This Lime Tree
Bower**, winner of the Guiness ingenuity
award, the Pearson TV writers residency
award, Meyer-Whitworth award, George
Devine award and Evening Standard
award for most promising playwright
(1996)

Melfi, Leonard
Hallowe'en (1973)

Mercer, David
In Two Minds (1973)

Meueller, Harald
Rosie (1977)

Miller, Danny
Jack's Out (1992)

Minton, Roy
Good Times (1973)

Minx, Paul
See How Beautiful I Am (2001)

Mitchell, Adrian
*Man Friday (*1973)

Moore, Ted
The Marshalling Yard (1989)

Mornin, Daniel
Kate (1983

Morris, Peter
The Age of Consent* (2002)

Moss, Chloe
How Love Is Spelt* (2004)

Motton, Ggregory
Looking at You (Revived) Again (1989)

Mr Pugh's Velvet Glove
Operation Wordsworth (1976)

Murphy, Gerald
Take Me Away (2005)

Murrell, John
Democracy (1994)

Neilson, Anthony
Stitching (2002)

Nemeth, Sally
Mill Fire (1990)

Neville, David Ian
Exile (1992)

Nkosi, Lewis
Malcolm (1972)

O'Brien, Flann
The Dalkey Archive (1978)

O'Brien, Maureen
The Cutting (1992)

Oglesby, Tamsin
Two Lips Indifferent Red* (1995)

O'Neil, Sean
Martin and John (1998)

O'Reilly, Kaite
Yard*, winner of the Peggy Ramsay
award (1998)

O'Rowe, Mark
Howie the Rookie*, winner of the George
Devine award, the Rooney prize for Irish
literature, Irish Times new play award
and the Herald Angel award for best
production at the Edinburgh festival
(1999)

Owen, Gary
The Drowned World* (2003)

Packer, Mike
A Carpet, a Pony and a Monkey* (2002),
Card Boys* (1999)

Pagan, Adrian
The Backroom* (1999)

Parker, David
The Collector (1972), *The Relief of Nartha
King* (1972)

Penhall, Joe
Love and Understanding* (1997)

Poliakoff, Stephen
City Sugar (1975), *Hitting Town* (1975),
The Carnation Gang (1974)

Polsky, Abe
Devour the Snow (1982)

Pomerance, Bernard
Someone Else is Still Someone (1974)

Pownall, David
Ladybird, Ladybird (1976)

Public Parts
The Marvellous Boy (1992)

Puig, Manuel
Mystery of the Rose Bouquet (1987), *Kiss of the Spider Woman* (1985)

Quick, Richard
Juvenalia (1976)

Rabe, David
A Question of Mercy (1998)

Raffo, Heather
*Nine Parts of Desire** (2003)

Rapp, Adam
*Blackbird** (2001)

Ridley, Philip
The Pitchfork Disney (1991)

Roche, Billy
A Handful of Stars, winner of the Plays and Players award for most promising playwright, the John Whiting award and Thames TV award (1988), *Belfry*, winner of the Time Out award for best play and Carling London fringe award for best play (1990), *Poor Beast in the Rain*, winner of the Charrington London fringe award for best playwright, Thames TV awards for best play and best production and the George Devine award (1989), *The Wexford Trilogy* (1992)

Rosagut, George
Travestie Aus Liebe (1974)

Rudkin, David
Ashes (1986)

Ryan, J Alexander
Would you like to be an Angel? (1976)

Sal's Meat Market
Charlie and Buck (1977), *I'm not walking* (1975), *Wild Animals from Memory* (1975), *Phil Teddy's Fun Palace* (1974), *Trouble on the Night Shift* (1973)

Scott, Milcha Sanchez
Roosters (1988)

Sentivany, Maria
The Magic of Pantalone (1973)

Shepard, Sam
The Tooth of Crime (1983), *Cowboys No 2* (1972)

Shill, Steve
Five Smooth Stones (1988)

Silas, Shelley
*Falling** (2002)

Silver, Nicky
The Maiden's Prayer (2000)

Simon, Mayo
These Men (1981)

Smith, Andy
Winter Visitors (1976), *Blood Red My Sunset* (1975), *Fist of Frozen Lightning* (1975), *The Insomniac* with David Camourai (1974), *Sawdust Caesar* (1974), *The Knockabout Punch and Judy Show* (1974)

Smullen, Eamonn
The Reprisal (1972)

St Clair, John
Stiff and Silent (1973)

Stephens, Simon
*One Minute** (2004), *Christmas** (2004)

Stock, James
Blue Night in the Heart of the West, winner of the George Devine award (1991)

Theatre Pur
Small Talk About Chromosomes (1993)

Thomason, Ed
The Double Man (1982)

Thompson, Brian
Turning Over (1983)

Thompson, Steve
Damages (2004)

Tidy, Bill
Fosdyke Two with Alan Plater (1977), *The Fosdyke Saga* with Alan Plater (1976)

Tinniswood, Peter
The Day War Broke But (1981), *Wilfrid* (1979)

Vonnegut Jr, Kurt
Happy Birthday, Wanda June (1977)

Wakefield Tricycle
End of the World Now (1975)

Walker, George F
Baghdad Saloon (1973)

Wallace, Naomi
One Flea Spare*, winner of the Susan Smith Blackburn prize (1995), *In the heart of America**, winner of the Susan Smith Blackburn prize (1994)

Walsh, Enda
Disco Pigs*, winner of George Devine award and Stewart Parker award (1997)

Wandor, Michelene
Friends and Strangers Alike (1974)

Ward, Nick
The Present (1995)

Watts, Murray
The Fatherland, winner of the LWT plays on stage award (1989)

Wells, Win
Gertrude Stein and Companion (1985)

Welsh, Irvine
Filth adapted by Harry Gibson (2000), *Trainspotting* adapted by Harry Gibson (1995)

White, Edgar
The Nine Night (1983)

Wilcox, Michael
Mrs Steinberg and the Byker Boy* (2000)

Wilkinson, Chris
Plays for Rubber Gogo Girls (1972)

Williams, Alan
Mean Streaks (1980), *The Cockroach that Ate Cincinatti* (1979)

Williams, Tennessee
This Property is Condemned (1975)

Wilson, Snoo
Sabina* (1998), *Darwin's Flood** (1994), *More Light* (1987), *Loving Reno* (1983), *The Number of the Beast* (1982), *A Greenish Man* (1978), *Vampire* (1977), *The Soul of the White Ant* (1976), *Everest Hotel* (1976)

Wilson, T Bone
Come Jubilee (1977)

Windsor, Valerie
Effie's Burning (1987)

Women's Theatre Group
Out! On the Costa del Trico (1977), *Work To Role* (1976), *My Mother Says I Never Should* (1975)

Woods, Keith
The Kid (1975)

Woolf, Henry
A Naval Occasion (1974)

Wymark, Olwen
Loved (1978)

Zajdlic, Richard
Dogs Barking* (1999), *Rage** (1994)

BOTTLE UNIVERSE

Simon Burt

Characters

DAVID (COCK DAVE), *fourteen*

LAUREN, *fourteen*

MR RICHMOND, *fifties*

Set

There are a few settings. The main one is Cock Dave's den/hole in the ground. It would be nice to realise the den as naturalistically as possible as it would make sense within the play that this place is the most tangible.

Of the others there is a wood, a bit of a classroom, grass by a motorway, a few stones from atop a Norman castle ruin, and an open grave.

This text went to press before the end of rehearsals so may differ slightly from the play as performed.

Scene One

Schoolteacher's desk. MR RICHMOND *is sat behind it reading a newspaper.* COCK DAVE *is sat at another desk, doing lines.* RICHMOND *looks up from his paper at* COCK DAVE, *checks his watch and then approaches him.*

RICHMOND. Hmm. Not bad handwriting for once.

COCK DAVE. Ta. Quite proud of it meself.

RICHMOND. Mmm. Pity it says 'I will not do my lines, you twatting bastard' two hundred times.

COCK DAVE. Well you can't have everything.

RICHMOND. Go on, you're done.

COCK DAVE. Y'what? You're still on the clock.

RICHMOND. I don't care. Go on, you're done. I'm going back to me paper, in peace for once.

COCK DAVE. Ey, I know your terms an' conditions. You're still on the clock and you're on the clock for another twenty minutes here, so cut out the not caring. We talk footie after I done me lines.

RICHMOND. Yes but you haven't really.

COCK DAVE. I'll do a few proper if you'll talk footie.

RICHMOND. Don't be bloody negotiating wi' me, lad. Bugger off.

COCK DAVE. But you like yer footie chats.

RICHMOND. I just want some peace an' quiet 'fore I head home.

COCK DAVE. You got monk on wi' me?

RICHMOND. No more than usual.

COCK DAVE. You have. Cos I threw that chair at Miss Cameron, isn't it?

RICHMOND. No that was the monk I had on with you yesterday.

COCK DAVE. It didn't hit her an' I never meant it to neither. I know what I'm doing, me.

RICHMOND. That was yesterday. Honest.

COCK DAVE. Oh. But you still talked footie wi' me.

RICHMOND. Aye. So do you believe me?

COCK DAVE. You in no rush to head home to Mrs Richmond then?

RICHMOND. Sod off.

COCK DAVE. But you like yer footie chats, you're only hurting yerself.

RICHMOND. I've no monk on.

COCK DAVE. So what were today's isolated detention for?

RICHMOND. I dunno. You just turned up. I assumed you knew why.

COCK DAVE. No.

RICHMOND. Well I don't either.

COCK DAVE. God's sake.

RICHMOND. But you always turn up.

COCK DAVE. I thought I'd still be in for Miss Cameron.

RICHMOND. No.

COCK DAVE. Oh.

RICHMOND. There must be something you've done.

COCK DAVE. Yeah.

RICHMOND. It be for that then, for all that swearing you done today. Now go.

COCK DAVE *starts to pack his few things away, really slowly.*

COCK DAVE. Ah well, makes no fucking difference to me. All me fucking classes are fucking isolations these days.

RICHMOND. You were in detention for that.

COCK DAVE. For what?

RICHMOND. All that fucking swearing.

COCK DAVE. You're still on the clock, I could report you for that.

RICHMOND. Yeah, see you in court. Now go!

At that moment LAUREN *enters, coat and bag wrapped around her.* RICHMOND *realises this is going to be awkward.* COCK DAVE *is incandescent.*

LAUREN. This is where you told me to come.

COCK DAVE. What's she doing here? (*To her.*) Fuck off, bastard face.

RICHMOND. Ey! Go! Hello Lauren. Don't worry. A few lines an' you'll be done.

COCK DAVE. She's coming into my detention?

She sits at a desk taking her coat off. He hands her a piece of paper. COCK DAVE *is offended.*

RICHMOND. 'Must not forget homework.' Fill that and you're done.

She starts to do her lines.

COCK DAVE. Fucking insult, this.

RICHMOND (*to* LAUREN). Ignore him.

COCK DAVE. This is my isolated detention, this. An' isolated means fucking isolated not bringing other cunts into it. You know how many folk I've twatted to earn this one on one thing me an' you have going? The graft I've put in?

RICHMOND. Ignore him.

COCK DAVE *kicks/throws a chair/table or something over with a crash. Lauren is scared.*

RICHMOND. Ignore him.

COCK DAVE. Aye, ignore me.

She nods.

You're nodding, you, not ignoring me, you dense bint.

RICHMOND. Ey!

COCK DAVE. Thought she were a smartarse. (*To* LAUREN.) Ignore me. Bad influence, me. That's why I'm in isolations. Cock of isolations, me.

RICHMOND. Oh do shut up. And pick it up.

COCK DAVE. Ey she's writing "Go fuck yerself go fuck yerself."

RICHMOND. Pick it up.

COCK DAVE. She is.

RICHMOND. Pick it up.

COCK DAVE. I'm not gonna an' you can't make me. An' you can't touch me.

RICHMOND *picks whatever it is up and puts it straight.* COCK DAVE *starts to leave but –*

RICHMOND. Look, you giving me shit is the biggest thrill of your sad little life, yeah? Well, bully for you. But you're not worth me getting angry, you isn't worth the blood pressure, lad, in fact you're not worth shit, lad. You've made yer choice, you think you're shit, so you are shit. You're a nothing.

COCK DAVE. Good comeback.

RICHMOND. Ta.

COCK DAVE. You want me to fuck off? Tell me to.

RICHMOND. I'm not gonna swear at you, lad. I isn't giving you excuses to hate me.

COCK DAVE. I don't need excuses.

RICHMOND. I'm not gonna tell you ought. Thirty years of teaching cocky buggers like you that think they know it all there's no point telling me there's any point telling you ought. Anyway, won't yer Mam be pleased to see you?

COCK DAVE. Don't start on her.

RICHMOND. Well then. Don't you mention Mrs Richmond then.

COCK DAVE. You wanna be careful what you say to me y'know. One day I'm gonna go to that room I saw on the telly wi' just the telly in it and they bring you yer food an' it's life of Riley in there.

RICHMOND. Yes yes.

COCK DAVE. I will. I'm gonna do what it takes to get there an' it be because you've pissed me off so much.

RICHMOND. You end up in clink it be no one's fault but yer own. Now go so I can waste me time on someone that's actually got a chance.

COCK DAVE. I were thinking of bunking tomorrow. But I be back in for me isolated detention with you.

RICHMOND *picks* COCK DAVE*'s lines up and screws them up.* LAUREN *sees this and looks at her own lines a moment before continuing.* COCK DAVE *leaves.* RICHMOND *looks at* LAUREN *a moment working on the lines.*

RICHMOND. Stop.

LAUREN. Sorry?

RICHMOND. Your lines. Stop.

She stops.

Just needed to make a point, don't work so hard you forget your homework.

LAUREN. No.

RICHMOND. I'm sorry I had to put you in detention.

LAUREN. That's alright.

RICHMOND. It isn't alright. But go on.

LAUREN. Sorry?

RICHMOND. Go. I want to read me paper. An' don't you need to be getting home? I hear you've got a home tutor.

LAUREN. How'd you know that?

RICHMOND. Your parents were saying about getting one at parents' evening. I'm not good enough apparently. Joke. They got one, didn't they?

LAUREN. Yeah.

RICHMOND. This tutor due tonight?

LAUREN. Yeah. She comes nearly every other night now.

RICHMOND. Well you best go then.

She starts to pack her stuff away. He retreats into his paper. She's about to go when –

LAUREN. My lines.

RICHMOND. What about them?

LAUREN. Aren't you going to tear them up?

RICHMOND. No.

LAUREN. You did his, in front of him.

RICHMOND. You're not him.

LAUREN. Why wasn't I in proper detention?

RICHMOND. Does it matter?

LAUREN. I want to be treated the same.

RICHMOND. You are being.

LAUREN. Then why wasn't –

RICHMOND. It wouldn't be fair to put you in proper detention with all the roughnecks with some of the stuff I've heard 'em say to you. They'd think all their birthdays had come at once. You'd just be a distraction, so best to put you in here with David's regular isolated thing with me.

LAUREN. I wouldn't mind. I don't pay any attention to it.

RICHMOND. Well it's academic. It's not like the likes of you are going to be in detention, is it?

LAUREN. No. Would you tear my lines up?

She passes him the barely started lines. He tears them up.

Thank you.

RICHMOND. This tutor that comes. How often?

LAUREN. Every other night now.

RICHMOND. Are they wanting you to change school?

LAUREN. How'd you know that?

RICHMOND. Not rocket science.

LAUREN. Yeah?

RICHMOND. What's the school?

LAUREN. It's the Queens one in town.

RICHMOND. Very good school. You want to go?

LAUREN. It means a right long bus trip.

RICHMOND. Oh it's the bus trip.

LAUREN. It isn't the bus trip.

RICHMOND. You'd pass their exam. You're a bright girl. And you wouldn't be the first from here to go there.

LAUREN. No? Would I be normal?

RICHMOND. Why do you want to be that?

LAUREN. Cos I do. I'd be a snob if I went there.

RICHMOND. How come?

LAUREN. My parents never believed in it 'til they worked out they had the money to send me there. They're snobs.

RICHMOND. You're the snob yerself thinking like that.

LAUREN. No.

RICHMOND. Yes. Your folks are just wanting the best for you. And it doesn't seem like I'm the best. But you just remember when they're saying stupid stuff to you, a few year from now you'll be going somewhere an' where will they be?

LAUREN. I don't know.

RICHMOND. Nowhere. That's where.

LAUREN. Yeah.

RICHMOND. You'll be fine.

He goes into his newspaper. LAUREN leaves.

Scene Two

The wood. LAUREN enters, still dressed as we last saw her. It is only a few minutes later. She sits and looks up into the trees trying to find something – finds it. Opens her bag and digs deep down inside it past books and pencils and lunch-box. Pulls out a length of rope. Looks at it in her hands. Undoes her collar and loosens her tie, starts to tie the rope around her neck. A few tears start to flow. She finishes tying it. Picks up the other end of the rope and stands looking up towards an unseen branch – at which point . . .

COCK DAVE (*off*). What you doing?

She nearly jumps out of her skin, stands there rooted to the spot, looking about, terrified, trying to find the voice.

(*Off.*) I said, what are you doing?

She finds the voice as COCK DAVE enters smoking, cockily hesitant.

He keeps his distance from her.

LAUREN. Nothing. Nothing. What, what are you doing?

COCK DAVE. I saw you leaving. Followed you to tell you to stay outta my fucking isolated detention.

LAUREN. Okay.

COCK DAVE. You best or I'll smack you, lass or not.

LAUREN. Okay.

COCK DAVE. Being a lass doesn't matter to me, equal opportunities an' all that.

LAUREN. Okay, I won't. Can you just go. Please.

COCK DAVE. What for?

LAUREN. Please.

COCK DAVE. Well no, you don't tell me where to be, you can't be in here either, cos I like to come in here an' have a smoke sometimes, specially when that cunt Richmond's doing me head in, an' he is cos of you today so you can fuck off out of it.

LAUREN. Okay okay, I'll go I'll go. Just a moment.

She tries to undo the rope but she has tied it too well. He starts to realise something is going on. It won't come off. She can't leave the wood with it tied around her neck. She gives up and looks at the ground not daring to look at COCK DAVE.

COCK DAVE. Thought you were going.

LAUREN. I will.

COCK DAVE. Well you're not fucking doing ought about it. I can't have me smoke wi' you here.

LAUREN. I just I just I . . .

COCK DAVE. What are you doing?

LAUREN. Nought.

COCK DAVE. Aye. What are you doing? It doesn't look like nought . . . if it is nought just fuck off out of here ey? Don't

want folk seeing me thinking I talk to bastard face. Go on,
fuck off.

LAUREN. I just wanna wanna . . .

*She breaks down and sits on the ground in a ball quietly
sobbing. He watches her, unsure, quietly freaked.*

COCK DAVE. Stop it. Stop it! Look, you doesn't have to go if
you'll stop. Yeah? You don't have to go if it isn't nought
you're doing you doesn't have to.

*She comes out of the sobbing just enough. She just sits there
staring straight ahead.*

*He sits several feet away from her, maybe lights another
ciggie.*

Well I've seen some fucking strange things in here when no
one's seen me. You know Neil an' Naz year above us? They,
they came in here, I saw 'em, they had a fight and then
wanked each other. What were that about?

LAUREN. I don't know.

COCK DAVE. They're fucking arse-bandits is what. Daren't
say ought though, they'd fucking have me. Things you see
in here. Only strange fucked-up folk come in here.

*Suddenly self-conscious of the rope again she tries to undo
it but fails again. Gets really agitated and frustrated this
time, different to her first attempt to get it off.*

Noisy. She sits there again defeated by it. COCK DAVE
realises what she was about to do.

You weren't kidding when you tied that.

LAUREN. I didn't mean to come to your detention. I wanted
to go to the proper one for everyone. Richmond made me.

COCK DAVE. Aye. Doesn't want likes of you mixing with the
mingers. Cunt. You want a fag, bastard face?

LAUREN. No.

COCK DAVE. They're good.

LAUREN. They're bad for you.

COCK DAVE. Well if you're off soon anyway. You not carrying on, then?

LAUREN. I'm not doing ought.

COCK DAVE. You are.

LAUREN. I'm not.

COCK DAVE. Am I meant to go screaming out of the woods for help or something? I not gonna. Carry on if you like.

LAUREN. I'm not doing ought.

COCK DAVE. Have I ruined it for you?

LAUREN. I just want this off.

COCK DAVE. You wanna hand?

She nods. He approaches her, both nervous of each other, he starts to untie the rope.

When I can get fags, which isn't that often, looking like a fucking bairn like I do, I don't give 'em to anyone, big deal this me offering you one, specially you being bastard face. An' you tell anyone I offered you a fag I'll kill you. Ey, you tied this good, wrong but good.

He pulls the rope away from her neck.

LAUREN. Owww . . . Is there marks?

COCK DAVE. It right red. It'll fade in a bit. Just look like you've had a time wi' some right randy cunt. Do yer shirt up it be fine. You gotta have a fag now I done that. I wanna see bastard face have a fag. If you serious you gonna be dead soon anyway so what's it fucking matter?

He lights and holds a cigarette out to her, she takes it, a little drag and coughs and splutters.

Knew you'd be fucking useless.

She puts it on the ground and stamps it out.

Ey, you bitch!

LAUREN. Sorry I –

COCK DAVE. You owe me now.

He throws the rope back at her, doesn't matter if it hits her.

An' I thought you were a smartarse? You need a slip knot to hang yerself.

LAUREN. A what?

COCK DAVE. Slip knot.

LAUREN. Slip knot?

COCK DAVE. I isn't that thick. I know stuff. That knot wouldn't have broken yer neck, just suffocated you, you daft bitch.

She gets tearful at her inability to get this right. He picks the rope up and holds it out to her. She snatches it and shoves it back in her bag.

'Doing nought', 'Doing nought.' Fuck's sake, who you trying to kid?

LAUREN. No one.

COCK DAVE. What attempt is it?

LAUREN. Me first.

COCK DAVE. Yeah?

LAUREN. Yeah. What?

COCK DAVE. Wow.

LAUREN. Wow?

COCK DAVE. It didn't look it. Right professional you looked. First attempt, serious you looked, kudos to you. You looked right hard about it. See it in me Mam y'see. She keeps going a bit funny an' trying to do herself but she fucking useless at it but keeps having a go every now an' then. Never fucking does it right though. And hanging yerself, yeah, kudos to you.

LAUREN. Your Mum's tried this?

COCK DAVE. No, pills, me Mam. Always pills. But ey you can't go wrong wi' hanging. That why you choose it?

LAUREN. Dunno.

COCK DAVE. Why not pills then?

LAUREN. Might not work.

COCK DAVE. What about yer wrists? Right ice cold water and . . .

LAUREN. Take too long.

COCK DAVE. In case you change yer mind?

LAUREN. Yeah.

COCK DAVE. An' you don't wanna change yer mind?

LAUREN. No.

COCK DAVE. No you do or no you –

LAUREN. I do wanna die. Well I dunno, but I do know when I get more frightened of dying than not dying it's . . . I don't like it, I don't like it at all.

COCK DAVE. Why?

LAUREN. I just don't . . . wh . . . why does your Mum want to die?

COCK DAVE. Dunno.

LAUREN. You don't?

COCK DAVE. She doesn't know.

LAUREN. But she must know.

COCK DAVE. Well, she fucking doesn't know bastard face, alright? You know why you wanna die, bastard face?

LAUREN. Cos people call me bastard face.

COCK DAVE. I don't call you bastard face much. Other folk say it much more than I do.

LAUREN. They do.

COCK DAVE. Yeah, they do. But I don't understand, you don't get upset when folk call you bastard face and stuff.

LAUREN. No.

COCK DAVE. You ignore it.

LAUREN. Yeah.

COCK DAVE. You never show ought.

LAUREN. No.

COCK DAVE. So what you doing this for?

LAUREN. I don't know.

COCK DAVE. But you don't do ought cos you don't give a shit.

LAUREN. I don't.

COCK DAVE. But it does hurt you?

LAUREN. Yeah. You must know it hurts me.

COCK DAVE. But why don't you say ought?

LAUREN. Cos I won't let you cunts know it does.

COCK DAVE. I don't say it as much as others, as like Katy and Sarah and Parma and Sam and Lisa and Rachel and Caroline and Louise and Manisha and . . . and all them. I'm not as bad as . . . your fucking fault, if you dead yerself making it our fault. You kill yerself it your fault, no one else's fucking fault . . . bastard face.

LAUREN. Okay.

COCK DAVE. Aye. Okay.

LAUREN. You're not a right worst one.

COCK DAVE. I isn't a Premier League one?

LAUREN. No.

COCK DAVE. Division Two?

LAUREN. One.

COCK DAVE. I wanna be in Division Two, or Three, Four or . . . It your fault. Doing nought when it does hurt, you stupid cow, it red rag to a bull, that. Thought you were a smartarse. You know nought about knots and hurting you. They two of the most important things you can know about, they are. Folk say stuff to me you know what I do? I fucking kick 'em 'til I get 'em down on the floor an' force their gobs open an' I gob down their throat an' tell 'em I got AIDS or cancer or something. You wanna do that.

LAUREN. No.

COCK DAVE. You should say.

LAUREN. I have said. Richmond bollocks folk an' they just carry on cos he's Richmond.

COCK DAVE. All them Premier League ones need protecting from you if you gonna do yerself.

LAUREN. I've not left no note though. No one'll know why.

COCK DAVE. Oh that's alright then. Well, it's not alright for me, I fucking know.

LAUREN. Soz.

COCK DAVE. I don't understand you, you don't show ought, you . . . You don't let folk fuck you up. You get me?

LAUREN. Yeah.

COCK DAVE. You don't let folk fuck you up!

LAUREN. How do I do that?

COCK DAVE. Cry.

LAUREN. What?

COCK DAVE. Cry! In class. In front of everyone. When they say ought to you. Big sobby blubby crying like you just done.

LAUREN. I couldn't.

COCK DAVE. Don't then.

LAUREN. You won't say to anyone, will you? Cos if you do I'll just do meself straightaway like.

COCK DAVE. I won't say to anyone.

LAUREN. Good.

COCK DAVE. I don't want folk knowing I been talking to . . . you.

LAUREN. I don't want folk knowing I been talking to you.

COCK DAVE. That's alright then.

LAUREN. Yeah.

COCK DAVE. Yeah.

She picks her stuff up and starts to leave. Stops.

LAUREN. Crying in class. What'll that do?

COCK DAVE. It'll headfuck 'em. Scare 'em. You wanna headfuck 'em?

LAUREN. Yeah.

COCK DAVE. Cry then.

She leaves.

Scene Three

Few days later. COCK DAVE wandering into the wood, lighting up a cigarette, making sure he is on his own. Satisfied that he is he pulls a phone out of his pocket, examines it – it isn't his, he's nicked it.

LAUREN. I did it.

Startled, COCK DAVE whirls round, standing up, trying to place the voice, he realises it came from above, he looks up to see LAUREN sat up a tree.

I did it.

COCK DAVE. What? You're a fucking ghost?

LAUREN. What?

COCK DAVE. You not dead?

LAUREN. No.

COCK DAVE. Should be, scaring shit out of me.

LAUREN. You scared me last time.

COCK DAVE. I ought to smack you. Kill you. Come down here.

LAUREN. No.

COCK DAVE. I'll come up there.

LAUREN. I'm stuck.

COCK DAVE. You got up there. What are you doing up there? You were gonna do *yerself*?

LAUREN. No, just thinking.

She pulls the rope out from inside her coat.

I don't know how to do that knot you said.

COCK DAVE. You want me to show you?

LAUREN. I did. What you said.

COCK DAVE. What did I say?

LAUREN. I cried. I did what you said. When they said stuff to me.

COCK DAVE. Oh. Good. What happened? You headfuck 'em?

LAUREN. I think so.

COCK DAVE. Told you. What were they saying to you?

LAUREN. Nought, just the usual. But I cried, proper crying. Couldn't believe I were doing it.

COCK DAVE. So what'd they do then? Them that were taking the piss?

LAUREN. Dunno exactly. I were busy crying.

COCK DAVE. That's no use, you've got to know what effect you're having.

LAUREN. It went very quiet, and all the whispering stopped.

COCK DAVE. Told you. You've headfucked 'em.

LAUREN. Good.

COCK DAVE. I thought you were a smartarse? Yeah? Y'see they might be in your head but you're in their heads, yeah? Cos they give you shit so they can laugh and laugh together but each one of them is shit-scared if they stop they'll become you.

LAUREN. Yeah?

COCK DAVE. Yeah. They're as trapped by it as you are. I'm not thick, me.

LAUREN. No you're not.

COCK DAVE. Whose class were it?

LAUREN. Richmond's. He doesn't hear much but when he does, he does bollock them, in front of everyone like but he does bollock 'em. Not that it does ought cos it's Richmond isn't it, they just laugh, but it's more than others do.

COCK DAVE. Well you're his favourite.

LAUREN. Isn't.

COCK DAVE. Are.

LAUREN. *Isn't!*

COCK DAVE. Did he talk to you after you'd cried?

LAUREN. Yeah, but not cos I'm his favourite.

COCK DAVE. No, folk do that when you do stuff like crying and being upset when you usually don't, specially if it doesn't look like you're specially looking for attention like, like you couldn't stop yourself from crying.

LAUREN. I couldn't stop myself.

COCK DAVE. Well then. It doesn't work for me that, crying and being upset, hasn't in years cos I'm always up to stuff.

First time I got nicked and I cried I got hanky, now I'm told to knock it off or they'll smack me. You've got a whole fucking piggy bank of attention stored up if you want it.

LAUREN. I don't.

COCK DAVE. I wouldn't say no to it. So what you thinking of doing yerself for if it worked?

LAUREN. Just thinking. I just wanted to tell you it worked.

COCK DAVE. Why?

LAUREN. Cos you told me. Cos no one's said ought to me for a few hours. It's alright.

COCK DAVE. You can't keep coming in here, this is my place this where I have me fags.

Her phone rings in her pocket, she takes it out, reads, her face crumples. She climbs down to the ground trying to keep herself composed.

LAUREN. Alright, I'm off, I won't come in here again.

COCK DAVE. What's on yer phone?

LAUREN. Nought.

COCK DAVE. I won't say.

She shows him. His eyes widen as he sees it.

They all like this?

She presses some buttons, shows him, he reads and reads and reads . . .

LAUREN. That's what crying's worth. A few shitty hours.

COCK DAVE. There's tons of 'em, fucking tons. Any cunt send me shit like this I do to them what they send me. What does Sandy mean?

LAUREN. It means I have a face that can sand wood.

He looks into her face a moment and then back to the phone.

COCK DAVE. Y'see, Sandy's good but most of these are so fucking obvious, cunt bastard face – easy.

LAUREN. Yeah.

COCK DAVE. What'd you keep 'em all for? Fucking stupid that.

She grabs the phone off of him.

LAUREN. I need them.

COCK DAVE. What for?

LAUREN. I feel quiet when I . . . I need them.

COCK DAVE. You're like me Mam, you.

LAUREN. Yer Mam?

COCK DAVE. Fucked in the head. You are gonna do yerself.

LAUREN. Yeah?

COCK DAVE. Yeah.

LAUREN. I dunno . . . I, I dunno what I want I wanna do. I don't know ought.

COCK DAVE. Well do you want me to show you the right knot?

LAUREN. Would you?

COCK DAVE. Do you want me to? You must know that.

LAUREN. I, I don't know I . . .

COCK DAVE. Well what do you fucking know?

LAUREN. I don't know I, I just know I don't wanna be me. I hate being me. I can't stand me. If I weren't me I'd laugh at me, I'd call meself 'bastard bastard cunt face'. I would. I'm so fucking useless. I should be able to find a way to make 'em stop. I should. I dunno what I wanna do, I don't wanna be me. I want to do something so mad, something so not me I'd never do it and I wouldn't be me anymore. That's what I wanna do.

COCK DAVE. Well, I do mad stuff.

LAUREN. Yeah?

COCK DAVE. Yeah. You wanna do something mad?

Scene Four

Traffic on a motorway roaring past. They're on the grassy verge.

LAUREN. What do we do?

COCK DAVE. You said you wanted to do something mad.

LAUREN. But this is . . .

COCK DAVE. If you're off soon anyway.

LAUREN. That's your answer to everything.

COCK DAVE. Cos it's fucking true. You wanna be not you?

LAUREN. Yeah.

He holds his hand out.

COCK DAVE. Trust me.

She takes it. He studies the motorway.

. . . Now!

They run into the darkness. The traffic reaches a cacophony including horns blaring at the. The cacophony fades. Lights up on COCK DAVE *and* LAUREN *laying flat on their backs on grass, head to head hysterically laughing and gasping for breath . . .*

S . . . S . . . See?

LAUREN. Y . . . Y . . . Yeah . . .

COCK DAVE. Told you it were mad.

LAUREN. My heart . . .

COCK DAVE. What?

LAUREN. It's going fast . . . oww . . .

COCK DAVE. How fast?

LAUREN. Like it's going to explode.

COCK DAVE. Cheaper than stuffing drugs up yer adrenaline. Lauren? Lauren?

LAUREN. . . . I'm listening.

COCK DAVE. To what?

LAUREN. My heart. I'm alive . . . I can't believe I did that.

COCK DAVE. Neither can I.

LAUREN. Haven't you done that before?

COCK DAVE. I can't believe you did it. Smartarse.

LAUREN. Minger.

COCK DAVE. Cow.

LAUREN. Twat.

They laugh more. A beat.

. . . What we just did . . .

COCK DAVE. Yeah?

LAUREN. The idea there weren't to die, were it?

COCK DAVE. No but if you –

LAUREN. If you're off soon anyway . . .

COCK DAVE. Yeah . . . I've had a few close ones doing that, but only to make me heart go faster. Not to die. Not like you, you're wanting yours to stop.

LAUREN. Yeah. So you don't want to die then, when you do that?

COCK DAVE. No, but it makes life more interesting if you might. They see you legging it across motorway an' they get their fucking loud horns going an' you're like 'Oh shit oh shit oh shit' –

They laugh.

Gets the heart going.

LAUREN. You were so crapping yerself.

COCK DAVE. I wanted to make sure you got across.

LAUREN. Then why'd you say leg it across in the first place?

COCK DAVE. To . . . to show you. Once one lorry went right over me.

LAUREN. What?

COCK DAVE. It fucking did.

LAUREN. It fucking did not.

COCK DAVE. It did.

LAUREN. You are so full of shit.

COCK DAVE. Don't believe me, I don't give a shit.

LAUREN. I believe you believe it did.

COCK DAVE. You want to do it again?

LAUREN. No.

COCK DAVE. Aye, first time is the best. Best keep memory of it, build up to next time like.

LAUREN. No, I just . . . no.

COCK DAVE. Are you sure you're suicidal?

LAUREN. . . . Well, am I like yer Mum?

COCK DAVE. Yeah. No . . .

LAUREN. What's she like?

COCK DAVE. She's me Mam.

LAUREN. I need to know, am I like her?

COCK DAVE. No.

LAUREN. No?

COCK DAVE. I just made you laugh, and happy? Yeah?

LAUREN. Yeah.

COCK DAVE. I can't make me Mam laugh.

LAUREN. No?

COCK DAVE. No that's what her pills are for, they make her happy, so she carries 'em around in this little fucking bottle in her bag like, reckon it's the fucking pills, what's my Mam is in a fucking bottle. I hasn't seen her all week. Hasn't come out of her room much this week.

LAUREN. You said she doesn't know why she feels like she does.

COCK DAVE. Aye.

LAUREN. I do know why.

COCK DAVE. Maybe you don't wanna die, mean I had to talk you into having a fag an' you're worried about being hit.

LAUREN. Well I don't wanna end up paralysed. Wouldn't be able to do meself then.

COCK DAVE. No.

LAUREN. No. You've got to be sensible about being stupid.

COCK DAVE. You're not wrong there.

LAUREN. How do you even figure out how to run across here in the first place?

COCK DAVE. There used to be a group of 'em drinking cider and legging it across here.

LAUREN. And you were one of 'em?

COCK DAVE. No, this were fucking yonks ago back when I were a bairn, I used to watch 'em from up under that bridge there. I did it once with them to show 'em I could but I cried so much they just laughed at me. But I'd done it the fucking cunts. So I just watched 'em from under the bridge wanting 'em to get hit. They never fucking did. Well not 'til Cock Poulton but that were years later.

LAUREN. What happened to him?

COCK DAVE. Oh he died. Aye it like you say, fucking dangerous this.

LAUREN. Did you see him get hit?

COCK DAVE. No. Wish I had. Story were he were cut in two an' that day he were right strange thinking he could smack cars coming at him. He turned into a right wanker just before he died. When cocks lose it, they doesn't half lose it. But before he lost it he were the best cock ever. You must remember him.

LAUREN. No.

COCK DAVE. He were cock when we were in first year.

LAUREN. No.

COCK DAVE. Best time were when he fronted up to this gobshite who couldn't hold his water being gobby saying he could be Cock an' it got round to Cock Poulton. Wannabe-Cock shat his load as soon as he saw Cock Poulton coming across the field at him just walking, like. Wannabe-Cock straightaway were cacking himself going back an' back on his little toddy legs far as he could an' still trying to give it some brass neck but he gets right to the Beck an' Cock Poulton still coming at him so he no fucking choice but to jump in the fucking Beck! Cock Poulton never even touched him an' he right smacked him.

LAUREN. If I were impressed by stuff like that I'd be right impressed.

COCK DAVE. Aye, respect, that's what I'll have.

LAUREN. Fear more like.

COCK DAVE. You saying I hasn't got respect?

LAUREN. No.

COCK DAVE. Cos if you are, I'll smack you.

LAUREN. Go on then.

COCK DAVE. Cock Poulton were right, you can't have everyone like you but you can have respect off of everyone!

LAUREN. Go on then!

COCK DAVE. I'm gonna have respect.

LAUREN. Yeah.

COCK DAVE. I'm going.

LAUREN. Okay.

COCK DAVE. Me Dad's on lates.

LAUREN. Okay.

COCK DAVE. I go watch telly wi' me Mam when he's on lates. I'm usually home by now even wi' isolated detention when he's on lates. She makes me a sandwich sometimes.

LAUREN. That's nice. But I thought you wanted to go to that room.

COCK DAVE. What room?

LAUREN. You said to Richmond you wanted to go to this room, and you'd do stuff to get there. Do you?

COCK DAVE. Aye.

LAUREN. Where is this room?

COCK DAVE. On the telly.

LAUREN. Where is it? Is it prison?

COCK DAVE. It is.

LAUREN. Why would you wanna go there?

COCK DAVE. On the telly it showed you just had a room wi' a telly in it an' they brung you yer food an' that were it. An' no one could get at you. No one.

LAUREN. Do you really wanna go there?

COCK DAVE. Sometimes. Sometimes I do. I really do. When me Dad does me head in an' I wanna stab him I think I could do. Me Dad fucks me off. I'm going. Me Dad's on lates. Ey, you best go an' all, police'll be coming.

LAUREN. Police?

COCK DAVE. Aye least one of them twats'll be on their mobiles blowing away to the pigs. What?

LAUREN. The people.

COCK DAVE. Where?

LAUREN. In the cars.

COCK DAVE. The twats.

LAUREN. No, the people. If we'd have been hit they'd have been – I didn't think of 'em I . . .

COCK DAVE. So?

LAUREN. I wasn't me. I've got to go. I'm going.

She starts to leave in a panic.

COCK DAVE. Ey!

LAUREN. I've got to go!

COCK DAVE. Ey no!

LAUREN. What?

COCK DAVE. Wait!

LAUREN. What?

COCK DAVE. If you isn't doing yerself tomorrow –

LAUREN. No.

COCK DAVE. I see you tomorrow?

LAUREN. . . . Yeah. What'll we talk about?

COCK DAVE. If you'll be here the day after?

She hurries away. COCK DAVE *just sits there, un-panicked, after a moment gets up and walks away.*

Scene Five

COCK DAVE *sat at a desk in the classroom.* RICHMOND *enters with some work/sheets for* COCK DAVE, *and a newspaper for himself.*

COCK DAVE. What you doing here?

RICHMOND. Just dropping yer work off.

COCK DAVE. But this isn't detention, this is isolated maths, you don't teach isolated maths. I thought Miss Cameron didn't have a monk on wi' me anymore?

RICHMOND. She isn't coming.

COCK DAVE. She only got to gimme some fucking work to do an' fuck off. She still got monk on wi' me over that chair?

RICHMOND. No she'd got over that. It's what you were doing at lunchtime.

COCK DAVE. Oh that.

RICHMOND. Aye that.

COCK DAVE. She isn't coming then?

RICHMOND. No.

COCK DAVE. You got me work then?

RICHMOND. Yeah but . . .

COCK DAVE. What?

RICHMOND. What's the point?

COCK DAVE. Gimme it.

RICHMOND. You won't do it.

COCK DAVE. I might.

RICHMOND. You won't.

RICHMOND *approaches him with the work-sheets in his hand.*

COCK DAVE. . . . Gimme it.

RICHMOND. No point.

COCK DAVE. I'd like to have the choice.

RICHMOND. Yeah, but I isn't giving you the choice.

> RICHMOND *tears the sheets up and lets them flutter down in front of him onto the floor/desk.*

Now shut up wi' yer whining. You can sit there.

> RICHMOND *makes to leave.*

COCK DAVE. What'm I meant to do just sit here?

RICHMOND. Yeah.

COCK DAVE. But I've no fucking work to do now.

RICHMOND. You wouldn't do it.

COCK DAVE. Aye but least I'd be not doing me work, now I'm just doing fuck all. What'm I meant to do?

RICHMOND. Sit there wi' the thoughts in yer head.

COCK DAVE. Bastard.

> RICHMOND *makes to leave again.*

. . . Ey! I'm talking to you! I'm here! I'm fucking here! You say come here, turn up an' then what? You cruel bastard.

RICHMOND. Cruel? Me cruel? Cruel is what I've heard you were doing to Katy in the yard at lunchtime. Screaming in her face, mock-punching her 'til she were crying, terrifying her, an' you laughing – laughing at her! An' you call me cruel? See how you like it eh?

> COCK DAVE *gets tearful.* RICHMOND *mock-punches him again and again.*

Oh see? You don't like it, do you? Do you?

COCK DAVE. No. Stop. Stop!

RICHMOND. You didn't stop for Katy, why should I for you?

COCK DAVE. Stop!

RICHMOND. Awww you upset? Poor little boy, rub it better. Mummy's big boy.

COCK DAVE (*quiet and tearful*). You cunt.

RICHMOND. Rub it, rub it better.

COCK DAVE. You fucking fucking cunt.

RICHMOND. Mummy's big soft boy.

COCK DAVE. You cunt.

RICHMOND. I've never hated you no matter what you've done, but doing that to Katy, to a girl who hasn't done ought to you, just cos you can. I do hate you now. You be under no illusions about that. You're scum, an' it's not your fault, really it isn't, but y'know, that's just tough on you, cos bigger picture like, you gotta make the best of a bad job like, like cancer, isolate it, so I'm gonna treat you like the cancer scum you are. An' I tell you this, you try to ruin the chances of someone, anyone who can make something of themselves an' I'll give you more of the same, Mummy's big boy. Think on it, Cock. An' pick this lot up before you go.

RICHMOND *leaves, newspaper in hand, the quietly sobbing* COCK DAVE.

Scene Six

Woods. A little after school. COCK DAVE *sat. Still.* LAUREN *enters.*

LAUREN. I been looking for you. Where you been?

COCK DAVE. You doing yerself today?

LAUREN. I wasn't planning on.

COCK DAVE. Okay.

LAUREN. You alright?

COCK DAVE. Yeah. You alright?

LAUREN. Yeah. You sure? You been in trouble?

COCK DAVE. I'm always in trouble.

LAUREN. Yeah.

COCK DAVE. No big fucking deal.

LAUREN. You're upset.

COCK DAVE. I'm not.

LAUREN. You are.

COCK DAVE. I'm fucking not.

LAUREN. Sorry.

COCK DAVE. I thought you might be right upset today.

LAUREN. No, I'm alright today.

COCK DAVE. Oh.

LAUREN. Sorry.

COCK DAVE. No no, if you isn't upset, you isn't upset . . .
    but . . .

LAUREN. Yeah?

COCK DAVE. But there were this picture on this phone I
    nicked today which were of you.

LAUREN. Yeah?

COCK DAVE. You know?

LAUREN. Well I were probably there when they took it.
    Whose phone were it?

COCK DAVE. Katy's?

LAUREN. She hasn't ever taken any pictures of me.

COCK DAVE. Oh.

LAUREN. What?

COCK DAVE. I got her up against the wall and screamed at
    her, telling her I were gonna smack her, I mock-punched her
    loads like, 'til she were, upset like.

LAUREN. She's not taken a picture of me.

COCK DAVE. Oh . . . But, but, but she has said stuff to you?

LAUREN. A bit. But she isn't one of the worse ones though.

COCK DAVE. She isn't a Premier League one then?

LAUREN. No.

COCK DAVE. Division One?

LAUREN. There's a lot of 'em. Definitely Division Two.

COCK DAVE. Near enough then.

LAUREN. You shouldn't have done that.

COCK DAVE. I didn't want to.

LAUREN. Then why did you?

COCK DAVE. Just did.

He's upset. She puts a hand out to him, touches him on the arm. He looks like death at her hand, frightened she moves her hand away.

LAUREN. Sorry. Don't smack or scream or hit or ought anyone cos of me. Please.

COCK DAVE. It were cos of you Richmond were a cunt to me.

LAUREN. Were he?

COCK DAVE. Aye.

LAUREN. What'd he say?

COCK DAVE. Stuff.

LAUREN. What sort of stuff?

COCK DAVE. Stuff about me Mam.

LAUREN. I'm sorry.

COCK DAVE. Don't want you sorry for me. Fuck you. You're a cunt. He's a cunt but he's a cunt that talks footie wi' me sometimes.

LAUREN. You like him.

COCK DAVE. I don't. He were just a cunt to me today. He were just like me Dad.

LAUREN. How were he just like your Dad?

COCK DAVE. By just being a cunt.

LAUREN. But what does your Dad do?

COCK DAVE. He says it's my fault me Mam's like she is, blames me, me being born an' all that. Like it's my fucking fault. He's the one who shagged her. I'm gonna go to that room, I'm gonna get there by stabbing him.

LAUREN. No you won't.

COCK DAVE. I will.

LAUREN. I'll hate you if you do. If you ever do.

COCK DAVE. Don't care what you think. The lad on the telly didn't want to come out of there, he were scared of coming out of there, that's how nice it were.

LAUREN. You don't wanna be scared.

COCK DAVE. No.

LAUREN. You'd be scared of coming out. You don't wanna go in there.

COCK DAVE. Shut up! This is your fucking fault! You doing me head in making me do things.

LAUREN. I haven't made you do ought.

COCK DAVE. You do.

LAUREN. You didn't say why you did what you did, did you?

COCK DAVE. No. I don't want folk knowing I talk to you . . .

LAUREN. Good . . . It's holidays next week. I can't wait. No school. It be brilliant.

COCK DAVE. Skiving's no fucking fun in holidays.

LAUREN. Where will you be?

COCK DAVE. About . . . Back field of your estate?

LAUREN. Yeah?

COCK DAVE. I'm in there sometimes, in holidays.

LAUREN. Okay.

COCK DAVE. Mum sometimes gets monk on wi' me being about all the time in holidays. Stays in her bedroom all fucking time.

LAUREN. I'll see you in the field sometime then?

COCK DAVE. Thought holidays be brilliant? What fuck would you wanna see me for in holidays?

LAUREN. My folks still do my head in. What do you do in the field?

COCK DAVE. Nought . . . I'm gonna go see me Mam.

He starts to leave.

LAUREN. Okay.

COCK DAVE. When me Dad's on lates we usually watch *Countdown* together.

LAUREN. You said.

COCK DAVE. Yeah cos that's what we usually do.

LAUREN. Okay.

COCK DAVE. She likes *Countdown*. I don't, it's shit. But I watch it.

LAUREN. Go see yer Mam.

COCK DAVE. I am. She makes me a sandwich sometimes if she isn't feeling too bad.

LAUREN. Yeah you said. That's nice.

COCK DAVE. Yeah it is.

LAUREN. Have you got a fag?

He passes her a fag.

I've nought to light it with.

He lights it for her and passes her it.

COCK DAVE. Me Dad's on lates.

LAUREN. Yeah.

He leaves, she smokes a little.

Scene Seven

A week later. The holidays. COCK DAVE's hole/den in the field he has dug-out. It is several feet deep, enough to stand up in, one area has a little polythene roof draped over a wooden frame. He's asleep. LAUREN enters, appearing at the top of the hole. They're both in casual clothes.

LAUREN. Hiya!

COCK DAVE *whirls round – she has come to his secret place.*

COCK DAVE. Hello.

LAUREN. Hiya. This is what you do in the field then?

COCK DAVE. Yeah. It's my place, this. It's only the first day of the holiday.

LAUREN. There's this tutor that comes.

COCK DAVE. A tutor?

LAUREN. A teacher that comes and teaches you in your home.

COCK DAVE. In your home?

LAUREN. Yeah.

COCK DAVE. In the holidays?

LAUREN. Yeah.

COCK DAVE. That's fucking evil that is. What's this tutor cunt teaching you?

LAUREN. Maths.

COCK DAVE. But you're the fucking best at maths.

LAUREN. They want me to be the best at maths ever like.

COCK DAVE. They want you to be cock of maths?

LAUREN. Suppose. Do you mind me being here?

COCK DAVE. You isn't doing yerself then?

LAUREN. . . . Right. Okay. Bye then.

LAUREN *starts to leave.*

COCK DAVE. . . . Are you . . . are you wanting to have a look at me den?

LAUREN. Do you want me to?

COCK DAVE. If you wanna.

LAUREN. How do I get down?

COCK DAVE. You sort of find your way down.

LAUREN. Right.

She climbs/finds her way down into the hole. He watches her.

It's quite roomy.

COCK DAVE. Aye. That's the bit to sit in. But I never do. Too busy digging.

LAUREN *sits in the comfy bit.*

LAUREN. It's alright. It can only get so big can't it, this hole?

COCK DAVE. It's something to do.

LAUREN. But it'll get silly if it gets too big.

COCK DAVE. I'll dig another one. Right next to this one.

LAUREN. You know, I believe you. First time I saw this hole from me bedroom window I thought it were subsidence.

COCK DAVE. What from?

LAUREN. The old mines round here, there's shafts under here
you know.

COCK DAVE. Is there?

He tests the ground.

LAUREN. Oh aye, well known that is.

COCK DAVE. You're taking the piss.

LAUREN. Don't believe me then. Plenty of houses round here
had subsidence problems.

COCK DAVE. That's all the trees there are. There's too many
trees.

LAUREN. Too many trees what?

COCK DAVE. Taking the water outta the ground, make it
flaky, the earth all crumbly like, pulling at the earth, nought
to do wi' yer fucking mine shafts.

LAUREN. Yeah?

COCK DAVE. Them houses they built right on the woods,
they got right cracks in 'em, that's the roots taking hold.

LAUREN. No way.

COCK DAVE. It's no dafter than what you're saying. It's well
known that is, about trees, you keep houses away from
trees. You hear all sorts hanging around like I do, better than
fucking books and numbers that is. I used to listen to these
builders like tutting and clicking their tongues at these row
of houses round here they were building. An' they were
right you know, this extension they were putting on, fucking
cracks everywhere now. That's why I haven't built me hole
anywhere near any trees.

LAUREN. Why would the trees cause your hole to fall in?

COCK DAVE. No. But I don't want to come across any
chuffing major tree artery like. Hard cunts them, need a
chuffing axe an' I be at it for days I reckon. Roses are bad
enough, their fucking roots, I dug one up to see how far its
roots went, me Dad fucking killed me tearing back grass up,

grass – fucking jungle more like. I tell you, you don't realise how far stuff underneath goes.

He hurries over to the roofed/comfy bit to show her.

This bit. I made it. When I say roof it's more of a tent like, really, but it does the biz. I've been in it when it's raining, nought gets in, honest.

LAUREN. Yeah?

COCK DAVE. Dry as ought it is under there. You don't believe me, do you?

LAUREN. Yeah I do.

COCK DAVE. I need it to fucking rain. Don't suppose you wanna sit in there and let me throw water over it?

LAUREN. I believe you.

COCK DAVE. You better.

LAUREN. Throwing water over it isn't a fair test anyway.

COCK DAVE. It can fucking take it.

LAUREN. But rain comes in drops doesn't it?

COCK DAVE. Yeah.

LAUREN. Not all at once.

COCK DAVE. Aye. You could sit in there and I'll piss over it, that's more like rain.

LAUREN. I don't see that happening.

COCK DAVE. I weren't gonna. But it's more like rain is pissing, that's why they say pissing it down.

She goes inside the comfy bit and sits down.

LAUREN. It's sturdy enough.

COCK DAVE. Huh?

LAUREN. Hard. Firm.

COCK DAVE. Course it fucking is.

LAUREN. I like it in here.

COCK DAVE. Do you?

LAUREN. Yeah. It's clever.

COCK DAVE. Weird seeing you, I mean yer clothes like.

LAUREN. Just clothes . . . Could I bring some cushions?

COCK DAVE. Cushions? Are you moving in or something?

LAUREN. It won't be comfy sitting in that all the time.

Points to the roofed bit of the den.

COCK DAVE. Does me.

LAUREN. Well you don't blumming think, do you?

COCK DAVE. This isn't a girl's hole wi' yer cushions.

LAUREN. I never said it were.

COCK DAVE. Are we going out?

LAUREN. What?

COCK DAVE. That's what folk do who go out.

LAUREN. What?

COCK DAVE. Argue about cushions.

LAUREN. No.

COCK DAVE. Best not be.

LAUREN. You said come here, though really I could come
here if I like cos you don't own this.

COCK DAVE. I made it.

LAUREN. I'm claiming squatter rights or something. You can
sit on the cushions if you like. Won't just be my cushions.

COCK DAVE. I'm not sitting on 'em, they'll be girl's
cushions.

LAUREN. Could I bring my dream-catcher too?

COCK DAVE. A frigging what?

LAUREN. A dream-catcher.

COCK DAVE. I know what you said, what is it?

LAUREN. Dream-catcher, to catch dreams – dream-catcher.
Ones in your sleep.

COCK DAVE. I haven't got any dreams.

LAUREN. Everyone dreams.

COCK DAVE. Only dreams I have are them wet ones –

LAUREN. David.

COCK DAVE. I don't want them catching, I want them.

LAUREN. No no, the dream-catcher brings the dreams to you.

COCK DAVE. So I'd have more? Yeah bring yer dream-
catcher here.

LAUREN. No not like, the idea is, it brings all sorts of dreams
from all over, collective unconsciousness like. Not just your
dreams. Everyone's dreams all together flying around in the
air together bumping into each other making new dreams
and coming back down into us.

COCK DAVE. What's it look like? If it's too girly it isn't
coming in.

LAUREN. No it looks alright, just looks like a couple of fancy
coat hangers really. There's fluffy bits to bring the good
dreams and these netty bits to keep the bad uns out.

COCK DAVE. So what you wanting to do with it?

LAUREN. Hang it up.

COCK DAVE. It'll look like a girl's hole.

LAUREN. Who cares?

COCK DAVE. I care.

LAUREN. 'Bout what?

COCK DAVE. 'Bout what folk'll think.

LAUREN. But no one knows about your hole, it's a secret hole.

COCK DAVE. It's still what I think they'd think if they did know.

LAUREN. But they don't know –

COCK DAVE. But if they did –

LAUREN. They aren't gonna unless you tell 'em!

COCK DAVE. Why would I fucking tell 'em?

LAUREN. You wouldn't, would you? It's a secret.

COCK DAVE. You can put it up, if you like.

LAUREN. Thank you. And cushions?

COCK DAVE. If you must.

LAUREN. I could make it nice in here.

It starts to rain.

COCK DAVE. Yes!

LAUREN. It's coming down.

Rain heavy on the den's placcy roof bit.

COCK DAVE. See? See? Fucking good roof.

LAUREN. Ey ey ey –

COCK DAVE. What?

LAUREN. Hang on a mo, let it start raining properly.

They wait a few moments as the rain gets heavier and heavier.

COCK DAVE. . . . Oh come on! It's pissing it down after a night on the piss now.

She inspects the den roof.

It's so much pissing it down it's a piss by a wall that can't wait to get out.

LAUREN. It's a good roof.

COCK DAVE. Told you.

LAUREN. You should show people this place – I mean if it weren't secret, show 'em the roof an' what you've done with it an' . . . it's good. You made it. You're gonna get wet if you stay out there.

COCK DAVE. Doesn't bother me.

LAUREN. You're gonna get drenched.

COCK DAVE. I'll smack it.

LAUREN. You'll smack rain?

COCK DAVE. Aye!

He tries to smack rain a moment. Stops. Bit embarrassed.

LAUREN. Looks like it's set in.

COCK DAVE. Aye.

LAUREN. Is yer Dad on lates?

COCK DAVE. Aye.

LAUREN. You gonna –

COCK DAVE. No, I'll stay here a while.

LAUREN. What you think I'm gonna do?

COCK DAVE. Dunno.

LAUREN. I isn't gonna do ought.

COCK DAVE. Best not.

He comes and sits in the roofed bit with her.

So you isn't doing yerself no time soon then?

LAUREN. No. Not in the holidays. You're not going anywhere, are you?

COCK DAVE. Not in the holidays. What we gonna talk about then?

LAUREN. Dunno. Nothing. Everything . . .

They sit there. It rains.

Interval.

Scene Eight

A few weeks later. The den has considerably 'girlied-up' with cushions and the dream-catcher and anything else appropriate. COCK DAVE *and* LAUREN (*back in uniform*) *are sat in the den. Not together side-by-side, they are apart but together in what they are doing.*

COCK DAVE *is reading one of her books, something slushy and trashy, something he so would totally not be reading. She is doing homework. He looks up from the book at her a moment and then the dream-catcher which he lingers on. She sees him looking at it.*

LAUREN. It does work, you know. I do have better dreams.

COCK DAVE. Aye, I've had better dreams.

LAUREN. Yeah?

COCK DAVE. It does work. You're working hard, even for you.

LAUREN. Yeah. Y' know it doesn't really work.

COCK DAVE. You said it does.

LAUREN. I mean it's just tricking the brain, but long as my brain thinks it does, it does work it gives me nicer dreams. Though I shouldn't talk about it much cos me brain'll realise.

COCK DAVE. Oh so it's just like a good blanket then?

LAUREN. A blanket?

COCK DAVE. Aye it's like my blanket I had when I were a kid. You've had me thinking all holidays an' new term it does something funny like, an' all the fucking time it's just a fancy blanket.

LAUREN. You had a blanket?

COCK DAVE. Aye.

LAUREN. You had a blanket?

COCK DAVE. It were called Noo-noo. Ey! I loved that
   fucking blanket! Always slept right good wi' that blanket. It
   just like that. Don't have to call it fucking poncey names
   and be all fancy dream-catcher like, but I know what you
   mean about yer fucking dreams.

LAUREN. Right. So how old were you when you stopped
   having a blanket?

COCK DAVE. Dunno, when I were a right bairn, when I were
   about ten.

LAUREN. Ten? You had a blanket at ten?

COCK DAVE. I never dragged it round the house wi' me or
   take it to school or ought. Not that it would have mattered if
   I had taken it to school cos I'd have smacked anyone who
   said ought. I just liked it there at night.

LAUREN. I bet it were right manky by the end.

COCK DAVE. It were minging.

She's back into her work.

So wi' yer nice dreams an' all that, now we back in school,
   like, you won't be doing yerself no time soon then? Mean
   you haven't mentioned it.

LAUREN. No.

COCK DAVE. You still getting shite?

LAUREN. Yeah.

COCK DAVE. So what's changed?

LAUREN. Dunno.

COCK DAVE. No. Well that's good then.

LAUREN. Suppose so.

COCK DAVE. Aye, cos Richmond, like . . .

LAUREN. What about him?

COCK DAVE. Well you're his favourite, like –

LAUREN. Isn't.

COCK DAVE. You are. An' he gets right funny when folk die. Like when that Matthew got ill an' snuffed it, like you that Matthew were, smartarse. Had right monk on, Richmond did. Didn't talk footie wi' me for a few weeks.

LAUREN. So what you saying?

COCK DAVE. Well FA Cup Final's coming up in a few weeks an' we always have right good chats about that an' the semis an' stuff like. You right spoil it if you go do yerself.

LAUREN. So you don't want me to kill meself cos Richmond won't talk footie with you?

COCK DAVE. Aye.

She goes back to her work. He tries to carry on reading her book, dismisses it and goes and does something to his den to distract himself from her. She watches him being all constructive a moment and then back to her work. He doesn't see this.

Scene Nine

School courtyard. There is a small tree which has been there a couple of years attached to a wooden pole/stake to support it. COCK DAVE enters as if hurrying to leave, he is all tears and yet trying to be full of attitude but failing. RICHMOND is following him.

RICHMOND. Now what was that about?

COCK DAVE. Nought.

RICHMOND. You can't say that was about nothing. You burst into tears. You.

COCK DAVE. I didn't.

RICHMOND. You did.

COCK DAVE. I didn't.

RICHMOND. You are!

COCK DAVE. I'm not. And anyone who says I am is gonna get it. Say what you'd usually say. Go on. Bollock me!

RICHMOND. Are you alright?

COCK DAVE. Bollock me!

RICHMOND. Well all they said to you were that you've talked to Lauren an' you started screaming at them.

COCK DAVE. C'mon, let me have it.

RICHMOND. You shouldn't ever speak to anyone –

COCK DAVE. C'mon!

RICHMOND. Or about anyone like you were just doing.

COCK DAVE. That weren't a bollocking. You can do better than that. Don't look at me like that. Fucking stop it!

RICHMOND. What?

COCK DAVE. Being nice to me.

RICHMOND. You shouldn't ever speak to anyone like you've just done. Thank goodness poor Lauren wasn't there you calling her all those names.

COCK DAVE. Start on about me Mam, you like that.

RICHMOND. David –

COCK DAVE. Do that.

RICHMOND. No.

COCK DAVE. Wuss. Now that was a good bollocking.

RICHMOND. What is it?

COCK DAVE. I didn't want to go back to class.

RICHMOND. That's what you're upset about?

COCK DAVE. I never wanted to go back.

RICHMOND. You had to.

COCK DAVE. Why?

RICHMOND. You've been behaving.

COCK DAVE. I thought you were meant to get rewarded for behaving?

RICHMOND. You have been.

COCK DAVE. Well I can soon sort that out.

RICHMOND. No no no –

COCK DAVE. Aye aye aye! It's fucked in there. I isn't me in there, I'm just stupid fucking hard cunt to everyone in there. It's all I'm allowed to be. It's weird and fucked in there. What's that about?

RICHMOND. It's called life.

COCK DAVE. Well fuck it. No one's themselves in there.

RICHMOND. I can't disagree with that. You still shouldn't start on folk like that just cos they say something daft to you. You're gonna get yerself into a lot of trouble if you do.

COCK DAVE. Well, they shouldn't speak to me like that.

RICHMOND. David –

COCK DAVE. Lauren. That's the worse fucking thing you can say to someone round here. They saying I talk to that smartarse cunt?

RICHMOND. Ey!

COCK DAVE. That bastard face?

RICHMOND. Shut up.

COCK DAVE. I'll have 'em!

RICHMOND. David?

COCK DAVE. She's a cunt, a cunt cunt cunt face a . . . a . . . a . . .

RICHMOND. Do you like Lauren?

COCK DAVE. That –

RICHMOND. Smartarse cunt face. Can we just take that as read – ey? Do you? Is that why you were shitty to Katy? Did you like her?

COCK DAVE *laughs at him.*

What? Something's bothering you.

COCK DAVE. Behaving's bothering me.

RICHMOND. It's bothering me.

COCK DAVE. Why am I?

RICHMOND. I don't know.

COCK DAVE. I don't either.

RICHMOND. How's your Mum?

COCK DAVE. Don't get onto her.

RICHMOND. I hear she's doing good at the moment, isn't she?

COCK DAVE. I hate that an' all.

RICHMOND. What?

COCK DAVE. That everyone knows about my family.

RICHMOND. You see the match last night? . . . You see it?

COCK DAVE. Don't start on the footie.

RICHMOND. Sorry?

COCK DAVE. I know footie's just softening-up barrage, like.

RICHMOND. It's no such thing.

COCK DAVE. Fucking is.

RICHMOND. Aye.

RICHMOND *holds out a cigarette to him.*

You can't smoke it here an' now of course.

After a moment COCK DAVE *takes it and it goes straight into a pocket.*

It were a good match though. Leeds'll be on their way back up.

COCK DAVE. In yer dreams.

RICHMOND. Their defence is back on track.

COCK DAVE. Mum's Mum.

RICHMOND. You behaving, it worries me you know. Mean it's good but it isn't the normal order of things.

COCK DAVE. Fucking isn't.

RICHMOND. It doesn't feel right.

COCK DAVE. Fucking doesn't.

RICHMOND. Look, you've just been caught fancying someone – like when you bollocked Katy. Can't you just ignore it? Have you been trying to talk to her? Ah well, you'll just have to keep away from Lauren if you don't want more of the same.

COCK DAVE. I'll talk to who I like.

RICHMOND. She doesn't need likes of you pestering her an' I really don't need you pestering her. Let it go.

COCK DAVE. Then get people to shut up saying I talk to her. You can't, can you? No one listens to you.

RICHMOND. You're way out of line.

COCK DAVE. What you gonna do? Saying I talk to her is one of the worst things they can do. What can you do that's worse?

RICHMOND. I'll think of something.

COCK DAVE. If she died you'd be right upset. Like when that smartarse cunt Matthew died.

RICHMOND. What you talking about him for?

COCK DAVE. If I died you'd be like when they planted that tree for Cock Poulton in the quad – nought.

RICHMOND. That's enough.

COCK DAVE. Nothing. When kids an' young teachers were blubbing there were nought on yer face but yer face.

RICHMOND. You what?

COCK DAVE. Like you couldn't get back to yer paper and fags fast enough.

RICHMOND. That isn't true.

COCK DAVE. I fucking saw you. An' you talked right loads of footie wi' me that afternoon they planted that fucking tree like nought had happened. When Matthew died you didn't talk to me for weeks in isolated detention.

RICHMOND. Didn't I?

COCK DAVE. No. I notice these things, you know. I isn't that fucking thick.

RICHMOND. No.

COCK DAVE. That's what I'd be if I died.

RICHMOND. I don't have favourites.

COCK DAVE. Bullshit you don't! An' if she died you wouldn't talk to me for ages.

RICHMOND. That's not true.

COCK DAVE. An' you know something? She can't fucking stand you.

RICHMOND. That's enough.

COCK DAVE. She thinks you're useless.

RICHMOND. Shut –

COCK DAVE. You sit there an' say nought when folk are giving her shite cos you think you'll make it worse an', an' she hates you for it. An' she is yer favourite an' she knows that an' they know that an' she hates you even more for it an' they do it even more an' you still keep on at her how better an' all she is, an' how to be more an' she hates you for it an' . . .

RICHMOND. . . . Are you done? . . . So you do talk to her?

COCK DAVE. She talks to me. She's the only one that does talk to me.

RICHMOND. What do you talk about?

COCK DAVE. Nought. Everything.

RICHMOND. We best go back in. You be alright?

COCK DAVE. Aye. What?

RICHMOND. You fuck things up for her and . . .

COCK DAVE *takes the cigarette back out of his pocket and holds it out to* RICHMOND *who takes it back.*

You know she's leaving, don't you?

COCK DAVE. How you mean?

RICHMOND. She's going to a school in town. She not told you?

COCK DAVE. You shit-stirring me?

RICHMOND. No.

COCK DAVE. She tells me everything.

COCK DAVE *runs off. After a moment* RICHMOND *goes back into the classroom.*

Scene Ten

Later that day. The den – it has 'girlied-up' even more. LAUREN (*in uniform*) *is sat in* COCK DAVE'*s den in the comfyish bit. She is doing a bit of homework, happyish for her. She doesn't see* COCK DAVE *arrive. He watches her for a few moments. She sees him.*

LAUREN. What?

COCK DAVE. I've decided I'm off.

LAUREN. Off?

COCK DAVE. To me room. Wi' the telly.

LAUREN. Why? What for?

COCK DAVE. Cos.

LAUREN. Cos what?

COCK DAVE. Cos.

LAUREN. No.

COCK DAVE. Am. What you think I should do.

LAUREN. No.

COCK DAVE. I reckon smash something. Shop front. Bin through window like. Something loads of folk'll see. There's that un where they hasn't ever selled me fags.

LAUREN. What've I done?

COCK DAVE. Nought. Just thought yeah, today's a good day for it.

LAUREN. Whatever it is I'm sorry but don't do that.

COCK DAVE. I could just smack someone in the street. See someone who does me head in. Luck of the draw an' all that. Someone old. That'll get me there. They don't like it when you hit old folk.

LAUREN. You're not hitting anyone.

COCK DAVE. I'll hit who I like. I'll hit someone who does me head in. You do me head in.

LAUREN. What?

COCK DAVE. Aye. You. You do my fucking head in.

LAUREN. Don't touch me. You ever touch me our friendship is over.

COCK DAVE. Friendship? You only talk to me cos you're miserable.

LAUREN. What?

COCK DAVE. Cos you're miserable.

LAUREN. I don't.

COCK DAVE. You do. You think I don't know that? You think I'm that thick? You do. It's all over yer fucking face. I know everything, me. Why would you talk to me?

LAUREN. Cos you're, cos you're alright.

COCK DAVE. I'm not alright, who do you think you're fucking kidding?

LAUREN. You are alright.

COCK DAVE. You wouldn't talk to me if you were happy.

LAUREN. But I am happy, talking to you.

COCK DAVE. But you only talk to me because you're you.

LAUREN. But I am me.

COCK DAVE. If you were someone else you wouldn't talk to me.

LAUREN. What does that mean.

COCK DAVE. I know what I mean. An' you won't be you for much longer.

LAUREN. I'm not gonna do meself. How many times do I have to tell you?

COCK DAVE. I don't mean that. You're leaving.

LAUREN. I were gonna tell you.

COCK DAVE. Smartarse posh school.

LAUREN. How do you know that?

COCK DAVE. Richmond says.

LAUREN. Why would he say to you?

COCK DAVE. Cos I said. You were doing me head in.

LAUREN. When?

COCK DAVE. Today.

LAUREN. But I hasn't seen you today.

COCK DAVE. That's what I mean. An' he were fucking me off so I said about you.

LAUREN. What for?

COCK DAVE. To piss him off.

LAUREN. I didn't want him to know. I don't want anyone to know.

COCK DAVE. I don't either. But they do. They've seen us an' everyone's pissing me off so why can't I piss someone off?

LAUREN. You can't.

COCK DAVE. Fuck that. I'm off. That room.

LAUREN. Don't.

COCK DAVE. I don't even like you.

LAUREN. I don't like you.

COCK DAVE. Things were alright before you.

LAUREN. No, they weren't.

COCK DAVE. No, but I didn't know they weren't. They've sent me back to class an' I can hear what folk say about you an' folk know I talk to you, I talk to cunt bastard face.

LAUREN. Sorry.

COCK DAVE. I'm wanting to smack meself for talking to you. It's doing me head in. I'm wanting to smack meself. I should. How do you smack yerself?

LAUREN. I don't know.

He tries to smack himself a moment. He doesn't get very far.

Stop it! You alright?

COCK DAVE. No.

LAUREN. Does it hurt?

COCK DAVE. Aye. I know me. I'll end up smacking folk cos of you an' Richmond won't stop 'em this time cos of you an' I'll get sent to special needs spacker school. All cos of

you. No fucking way. That room. I wanna be there now.
Aye, gotta do something. Gotta do something.

LAUREN. David –

COCK DAVE. Now!

LAUREN. What've they sent you back to class for?

COCK DAVE. Cos I've been behaving! That's your fault, that
is.

LAUREN. I'm sorry.

COCK DAVE. What you care? Posh school. You'll meet other
smartarse posh twats. You'll become someone else.

LAUREN. I won't.

COCK DAVE. You will.

LAUREN. We don't see each other at school as it is, only here,
we can just stay as we are. And I definitely won't want to be
doing myself anymore.

COCK DAVE. You won't need me.

LAUREN. I will.

COCK DAVE. Why will you?

LAUREN. I don't know.

COCK DAVE. You'll meet other smartarse twats. You'll
become someone else.

LAUREN. I won't.

COCK DAVE. You will.

LAUREN. Ey! Me parents'll still do me head in.

COCK DAVE. Will they?

LAUREN. Yeah.

COCK DAVE. You sure?

LAUREN. Course they will. They always will. So I'll still need
to come here, won't I? I'll still need you.

COCK DAVE. Will you?

LAUREN. Yeah.

COCK DAVE. You promise?

LAUREN. Promise. Ey, you want to go and do something really –

COCK DAVE. Mad? Fuck yeah. Yeah lets. Now.

LAUREN. No. Calm?

COCK DAVE. Calm? What do you mean?

Scene Eleven

The top of a Norman castle ruin. A cluster of ancient masonry, sprouting grass, a vast blue sky – the top of the world, for round here anyway. The sun beats down. The air is so clear and fresh. LAUREN's hand appears over the crest of the peak, grips on, hauls herself up. COCK DAVE follows, much more out of breath than she is. LAUREN is more familiar with the brickwork than he is and knows exactly where to sit.

LAUREN. You're out of puff.

COCK DAVE. It's fucking long way up that.

LAUREN. Here's something else that'll take yer breath away – look.

She looks out. He still has his head down.

You can see everything, the whole chuffing universe. All the estates, shops, lakes, the motorway's like a blumming snake.

COCK DAVE. . . . Wow.

LAUREN. You never been up here before?

COCK DAVE. Well, it's an old castle, isn't it?

LAUREN. So?

COCK DAVE. Old – boring.

LAUREN. Doesn't that make it more interesting though?

COCK DAVE. No, everything that's gonna have happened in it an' to it has happened.

LAUREN. This has been here nearly a thousand years.

COCK DAVE. It were for the posh folk.

LAUREN. The Normans that invaded us. Well I say us, I could be a descendant of a Norman so us is kind of daft.

COCK DAVE. An' what'd I be?

LAUREN. How'd you mean?

COCK DAVE. Well, I'm British, isn't I?

LAUREN. You'd be a Saxon.

COCK DAVE. Them that were here 'fore fucking Normans arrived?

LAUREN. Yeah. Or you could be the Norman an' I could be the Saxon. Normans were the ones who did the invading and liked to fight.

COCK DAVE. Does it matter?

LAUREN. This castle up here away from everyone, the posh folk looking down over everyone all shut away in their castle. Nought changes. Mind you the Saxons would have murdered the lot of 'em given half a chance so . . . What are you looking at?

COCK DAVE. The sky. This isn't fair. When I go looking for places to be on me own I end up under a motorway bridge. You find somewhere an' it's . . .

LAUREN. What? You wanted to see 'em run across the motorway.

COCK DAVE. First time I went there I were only a bairn, just wanting to be on me own. Dad doing me head in.

LAUREN. I don't like your Dad.

COCK DAVE. I had been smashing the glass in the phonebox, so he were right wanting to smack me that time.

LAUREN. What you smash it for?

COCK DAVE. Cos the bloke that came an' fixed it'd talk to me while he fixed it. So I kept smashing it so he'd come an' fix it. Police found out so me Dad found out. So I found under the motorway bridge, an' them that ran across. You're much better at finding places than me.

LAUREN. I've only been here when we were studying it. I've never come here on me own. I just stay in me room, me. But is good, isn't it?

COCK DAVE. Aye.

LAUREN. Bit like running across the motorway.

COCK DAVE. You know what . . . it is a bit. It is a bit . . .

LAUREN. Can you feel your heart going?

COCK DAVE. Aye a bit. Everything's so fucking small.

LAUREN. We're like giants. Ey, look at this –

She gets up right beside him and puts her hand out in front of his eye-line.

I've got the supermarket in the palm of me hand, and –

She screws her hand up and makes an exploding sound.

Gone.

Moves her hand to another angle, his eyes follow.

And the farmhouse there –

She makes a pinching gesture as if she is picking it up.

I've pulled it out of the earth, scooped it out and I'm dropping it . . . and . . .

Makes an explosion sound.

COCK DAVE. Fucking hell, you can be violent when you want to be.

Her hand moves again, his eyes follow . . . a moment of silence as they both follow the eye-line.

. . . The school.

She screws her hand up again and again and again with a vicious explosion sound.

She drops her hand and stares hatred towards it for a moment . . . she looks at COCK DAVE, *there is a very quick momentary mutual kiss on the lips. She sits back down on the ancient brick a moment, a bit embarrassed.* COCK DAVE *keeps looking out – spots something and puts his hand out making a pinching gesture and a screeching sound for a few moments.*

LAUREN. What you doing?

COCK DAVE. Motorway pile-up.

LAUREN. You nasty bugger.

COCK DAVE. This coming from someone who's just nuked half the valley. Ta for showing me this.

LAUREN. You're alright.

COCK DAVE. It's alright this . . . I believe you, you know. When you say you'll stay being me friend. I believe you.

LAUREN. Thank you.

COCK DAVE. Yeah this is better than the motorway. All those mad things I were gonna show you, dive-bombing the lake like from this ledge, I don't think I'll bother.

He looks at his watch.

LAUREN. You go to go?

COCK DAVE. No.

LAUREN. Go be with yer Mum if you wanna.

COCK DAVE. I wanna be with you.

LAUREN. You don't have to be with me all the time. I'm alright, you know. I'm not going to do meself. I thought we'd –

COCK DAVE. Well you would say that if you were going to.

LAUREN. Ey. I thought we were past all that.

COCK DAVE. Soz.

LAUREN. If it gonna make you feel bad, go watch telly wi' her and let her make you sandwiches.

COCK DAVE. She does me head in.

LAUREN. Mine do my head in. You don't have the monopoly on head-doing-in, you know.

COCK DAVE. No. An' there's detention you know, well not that I am on detention but me an' Richmond still like to talk footie and –

LAUREN. Well go then.

COCK DAVE. I don't wanna.

LAUREN. Then what you –

COCK DAVE. I'm saying, I don't want to.

LAUREN. Oh . . .

They look as if they are about to kiss again, they get a bit too embarrassed and instead turn outwards to the valley, their arms outstretched and mime destroying things with their hands making explosion sounds . . .

Scene Twelve

School corridor/yard/quad or something.

COCK DAVE. What you got me out here for now? This is harassment now, this!

RICHMOND. I need to speak to you.

COCK DAVE. Aye an' I know what fucking about.

RICHMOND. No.

COCK DAVE. I do. What's detention gonna be for this time? I hasn't fucking done ought an' you know it.

RICHMOND. No you don't –

COCK DAVE. I could complain about you y'know. All these detentions like just to keep me away from Lauren.

RICHMOND. They were deserved.

COCK DAVE. Pull the other one. Aye.

RICHMOND. It's not about that –

COCK DAVE. You do admit it!

RICHMOND. I do need to speak to you –

COCK DAVE. You being sly like. I'll put complaint in about you.

RICHMOND. Do what you like I still need to speak to you.

COCK DAVE. She still talks to me, you know, despite all the times you've put me in detention for sweet FA. An' anyway I'd talk to her now just to give you monk on. I'd have talked to her years ago if I'd known it give monk on.

RICHMOND. Will you let me speak? For God's sake, lad! Shut up!

COCK DAVE. What's it about?

RICHMOND. Your Mum.

COCK DAVE. Don't get started on her.

RICHMOND. I'm not –

COCK DAVE. I know you!

RICHMOND. No you don't.

COCK DAVE. I do.

RICHMOND. I'm not having a go.

COCK DAVE. You be trying all that how I'm not spending enough time wi' her now I got Lauren. Try ought you.

RICHMOND. David, no –

COCK DAVE. To make me feel bad? You isn't getting ought past me.

RICHMOND. David.

COCK DAVE. She doesn't bloody say ought to me when I am there, even when her bloody pills are doing the job so that isn't going to work on me.

RICHMOND. Don't be saying that.

COCK DAVE. So nought's gonna work on me to keep me away from yer precious Lauren. She gonna talk to me even when she goes to posh school. She promised me.

RICHMOND. She shouldn't have done that.

COCK DAVE. There's nought you can do or say that's gonna stop me yakking to Lauren. Not a fucking thing.

RICHMOND. You know you're your own worst enemy, you.

COCK DAVE. Aye.

RICHMOND. You make things so hard.

COCK DAVE. What is it? What is it? Do yer worst. I can take it.

RICHMOND. Your Mum's died. I had a phonecall from yer Dad, he wanted me to tell you.

Maybe RICHMOND *puts a hand on the boy's arm for a moment, something physical.* COCK DAVE *shrugs it or glares it away or something.*

COCK DAVE. It's FA Cup Final this weekend.

RICHMOND. It is.

COCK DAVE. We always have good talks about that.

RICHMOND. We do.

COCK DAVE. I get meself put in your detention espec.

RICHMOND. We can if you want to.

COCK DAVE. I might not want to.

RICHMOND. No.

COCK DAVE. Me Mam, I isn't surprised.

RICHMOND. No.

COCK DAVE. Not surprised surprised.

RICHMOND. No.

COCK DAVE. He say how she . . . ?

RICHMOND. No.

COCK DAVE. Hanging I bet. Or something. But not pills. Could never get pills to do it. What you think?

RICHMOND. I don't know. Shall I drive you home?

COCK DAVE. Why?

RICHMOND. I think you –

COCK DAVE. There's nought there. He'll fuck off, you wait. Won't see him for dust. Why you think he got you to tell me? You know something, you're a fucking cunt, Richmond, but he shouldn't have got you to do that. He's more of a cunt than you'll ever be.

RICHMOND. Thank you.

COCK DAVE. Suppose it just weren't meant a be. Us talking about FA Cup this year.

RICHMOND. That doesn't matter.

COCK DAVE. Does to me. She might as well have died, just thought it'd be you wi' the monk on, not me.

RICHMOND. What you talking about?

COCK DAVE. Weren't meant a be.

RICHMOND. David, she has died.

COCK DAVE. Not her, *her* – Lauren. Dead or alive we isn't talking FA Cup this year. It hasn't mattered one way or the fucking other.

RICHMOND. Why should Lauren be dead?

COCK DAVE. Cos of all what folk say to her.

RICHMOND. What was she gonna . . . she was gonna . . . ?

COCK DAVE. If she had have done, if she had have done, if
she had have done, my Mam'd . . .

RICHMOND. I didn't know that.

COCK DAVE. Me Mam . . .

RICHMOND. Ey, now you don't know that.

COCK DAVE. If she had have done . . .

RICHMOND. How serious was she?

COCK DAVE. I bet it's a really good final this year an' all.

RICHMOND. I know it's not a good time but you must tell
me. How serious was she?

COCK DAVE. The best.

RICHMOND. Best what?

COCK DAVE. Best final.

RICHMOND. You don't know that, but look, Lauren –

COCK DAVE. I saved her.

RICHMOND. She's alright?

COCK DAVE. Aye she talked to me. I were there when she
were gonna an' we talked an' stuff an' I saved her. I did I . . .
Me. But me Mam, she . . .

RICHMOND. David, tell me, she's not still wanting to kill
herself? David? David? Please.

COCK DAVE *smiles a horrible smile.*

What you smiling for?

COCK DAVE. Me Mam, she did bloody love me.

RICHMOND. Of course she did.

COCK DAVE. That's why she – she missed me! Ha! Got her!

RICHMOND. David . . .

COCK DAVE. I win!

COCK DAVE *leaves.*

Scene Thirteen

The den. COCK DAVE *is sat there wearing a muddied dirty uniform/shirt. Some of the cushions are covered in mud, the dream catcher is broken/smashed. The place has been trashed.*

LAUREN *appears at the top of the hole, upset and angry, but a different kind of upset from the suicide upset, and she doesn't notice what has happened to the den, all caught up in herself.*

LAUREN. You said! Oi! You hear me, you bastard! You said! It must have been you you're the only one who knows all that's been thrown at me this afternoon. Had Richmond all bloody nice an' everything an' then I got it in the neck from headmaster for not saying. It my fault he no fucking control. Oi!

COCK DAVE. What?

LAUREN. You said.

COCK DAVE. Aye.

LAUREN. Everyone knows I were bullied.

COCK DAVE. Aye.

LAUREN. But everyone knows.

COCK DAVE. Everyone knew anyway.

LAUREN. But they didn't know that they knew. It wasn't . . . They do now!

COCK DAVE. What?

LAUREN. It's humiliating! No one knew. No one. You told them. It were our secret. Why?

COCK DAVE. It just came out.

LAUREN. Just came out?

COCK DAVE. Aye. Soz.

LAUREN. Soz?

COCK DAVE. Didn't mean to.

LAUREN. Too late.

COCK DAVE. I don't give a shit.

LAUREN. I hate you.

COCK DAVE. I hate you.

LAUREN. I can't wait to leave now.

COCK DAVE. Good.

LAUREN. Yeah, can't wait to get to posh private snobby school. Fuck the lot of you. And fuck you.

COCK DAVE. You go then.

LAUREN. I will. I am. Few days an' I'm off.

COCK DAVE. Aye.

LAUREN. Gone.

COCK DAVE. You go become someone else. That what you want, isn't it?

LAUREN. I wouldn't have.

COCK DAVE. You would.

LAUREN. Well, I will now, yeah. I will. Fuck it. I told you I wouldn't have. Why couldn't you believe me?

COCK DAVE. Cos I don't.

LAUREN. Oh. You didn't have to do that. You've humiliated me worse than any fucking bullying ever has.

COCK DAVE. Good.

LAUREN. Fuck you.

COCK DAVE. It did just come out, I didn't mean it to, it just . . . fuck you.

LAUREN. What's happened to our place?

She climbs down into it.

Has someone found it?

COCK DAVE. There's a hole in the roof.

LAUREN. A hole in the roof couldn't do this.

She picks up the broken dream-catcher.

You did this? Why?

COCK DAVE. It just happened. Soz.

LAUREN. You've trashed it.

COCK DAVE. Yeah, course I have. Posh twat. Bastard face.

LAUREN. Why are you being like this?

COCK DAVE. Dunno. Cos you'll get posh mates. Cos you do
me head in. I should give you shit. Aye I should. I should!

LAUREN. No.

COCK DAVE. Bastard face. You'd only have done what me
Mam's done anyway.

LAUREN. Why, what's yer Mam done? . . . She done it?

*She squeezes his hand or something, again he pulls away
from it totally.*

COCK DAVE. Like you will.

LAUREN. No.

COCK DAVE. You won't mean to.

LAUREN. Stop it.

COCK DAVE. What?

LAUREN. You're scaring me.

COCK DAVE. You won't be able to stop yerself.

He smashes the dream-catcher some more.

I shouldn't have stopped you.

LAUREN. Yeah you should.

COCK DAVE. I wish you were dead.

LAUREN. When's the funeral?

COCK DAVE. Things'd be alright if you were dead.

LAUREN. When's the funeral?

COCK DAVE. Dunno. I isn't going.

LAUREN. You must go.

COCK DAVE. Fucking isn't.

LAUREN. I'll go with you.

COCK DAVE. What for?

LAUREN. Cos.

COCK DAVE. I'm not having folk know I go around with you.

LAUREN. David –

COCK DAVE. No!

LAUREN. It doesn't matter now.

COCK DAVE. It fucking does. I'm gonna be Cock Dave, me. I don't talk to minging cunt bastard faces like you. I'm me! Me! Your fault!

LAUREN. David, please –

If it feels earned he should really get hold of her and scream in her face here so there's no escape from his bile.

COCK DAVE. *Your fault!* Fuck off bastard cunt face!

She leaves him in the trashed den.

Scene Fourteen

The funeral. COCK DAVE *is stood in a shirt and a black tie. A* VICAR *is reading the words as the coffin is lowered. A few yards behind him is* RICHMOND *in the requisite suit and tie, he might be carrying his anorak under his arm. The* VICAR *continues. As he reaches the end in the background unseen to* COCK DAVE *and the teacher* LAUREN *enters, in her new school uniform, she watches. The* VICAR *finishes. People start to leave.* RICHMOND *is wanting to approach but stops as he sees* LAUREN *approaching* COCK DAVE. *He watches.*

COCK DAVE. Your uniform.

LAUREN. Yeah. What do you think?

COCK DAVE. Uniform's a uniform.

LAUREN. It were a good service.

COCK DAVE. Were it? Never been to a funeral before.

LAUREN. I have. Yeah.

COCK DAVE. I wouldn't want to be buried.

LAUREN. Me neither it's . . .

She looks down into the hole.

How are you doing?

COCK DAVE. Alright.

LAUREN. You seem calmer.

COCK DAVE. Doctor's given me these pills to take.

LAUREN. What?

COCK DAVE. I've got me own now just like me Mam.

LAUREN. No.

COCK DAVE. S'alright. I hasn't taken 'em.

LAUREN. No you must.

COCK DAVE. S'alright. I don't need 'em.

LAUREN. If they say take your pills you take 'em.

COCK DAVE. Well I'm not. How's it at posh school then?

LAUREN. Alright.

COCK DAVE. Just alright?

LAUREN. Good. Really good. Really really good.

COCK DAVE. See? Said.

LAUREN. Yeah. You did.

He starts to leave, she stays by the grave.

COCK DAVE. Bye then, cunt face.

LAUREN. Bye.

As he leaves RICHMOND *gets in his way.*

RICHMOND. Ey, if you've nought doing later how about an isolated detention an' we'll talk footie for a bit an' then I'll drive you back to the home. You fancy that?

COCK DAVE. Not really.

RICHMOND. Well the offer's there if you like. I'll be there, same old classroom, same old newspaper, you know where I'll be, if you . . .

COCK DAVE. What you come for?

RICHMOND. I was the one who told you.

COCK DAVE. Only cos me Dad's a cunt, that's nought to do wi' you.

RICHMOND. No I just thought I, we've talked about footie a lot down the years.

COCK DAVE. So?

RICHMOND. How's the home working out?

COCK DAVE. It's a home.

RICHMOND. So where are you going now?

COCK DAVE. Home.

RICHMOND. The home?

COCK DAVE. No.

RICHMOND. But you don't live there any more.

COCK DAVE. Lauren.

RICHMOND. What about her?

COCK DAVE. You were right.

RICHMOND. I might see you this afternoon then?

COCK DAVE *just leaves* RICHMOND *standing there. He approaches* LAUREN *still stood at the graveside.*

What are you doing here?

LAUREN. Nought.

RICHMOND. Shouldn't you be at school?

LAUREN. I'm just going.

RICHMOND. Ey, hang on.

LAUREN. What?

RICHMOND. How's it working out? How's it going?

LAUREN. Alright.

RICHMOND. How's the work? Harder?

LAUREN. Yeah.

RICHMOND. And are you average?

LAUREN. Yeah.

RICHMOND. Good.

LAUREN. Yeah.

RICHMOND. I know you and him were friends.

LAUREN. Yeah. We weren't y'know.

RICHMOND. He says you were. First time I thought ought were wrong wi' you when I heard you an' him were talking. And you're here today.

LAUREN. Well it's his Mam, isn't it?

RICHMOND. Aye.

LAUREN. Bye.

RICHMOND. Lauren. When you left, you didn't say goodbye when you left. You just left.

LAUREN. Yeah.

RICHMOND. I just thought you'd have said goodbye to me.

LAUREN. You didn't tell me his Mam had done it, made me think he'd just dobbed me.

RICHMOND. It just came out as he were upset.

LAUREN. You just started pulling people out of class an' bollocking 'em like mad an' then headmaster bollocking me . . .

RICHMOND. The headmaster shouldn't have blamed you for not saying, it were my fault, I should have explained to him quicker, it wasn't your fault.

LAUREN. But I were leaving anyway, what did it matter?

RICHMOND. I don't know. It needed saying.

LAUREN. But you'd heard it for months an' months before.

RICHMOND. Well, if it were upsetting you. An' I didn't want to embarrass you, make it worse, and you never said, the headmaster shouldn't have but, but he had a point, he . . .

LAUREN. Yeah.

RICHMOND. Yes and . . .

LAUREN. Okay.

RICHMOND. David says you hate me. Is that just David being David or . . . You didn't say goodbye. Do you hate me?

LAUREN. I hate lots of people.

RICHMOND. David said you'd thought of killing yourself.

LAUREN. What? No.

RICHMOND. But you thought about it?

LAUREN. I might have said something but, he were only worried cos you'd have monk on if I were dead cos he likes to talk footie wi' you.

RICHMOND. Yes.

LAUREN. It wasn't a very good turn-out.

RICHMOND. I suppose not.

LAUREN. He'll have liked you coming. He might not say but, honest. I suppose it's difficult for his Mam to have known many folk if she never really talked to anyone much.

RICHMOND. Lauren, I'm sorry.

LAUREN. What for?

RICHMOND. No, I am sorry.

LAUREN. Yeah.

RICHMOND. No Lauren I –

LAUREN. I've got to go now.

RICHMOND. Yes. Yes, you should. Well I hope things work out for you. I'm glad you're average.

LAUREN. He'd never say and I don't think he even knows himself but, but he thinks the world of you. David. You're more of a Dad to him than his Dad ever was. You're still crap but you're a better Dad than . . . Will you tell him he must take his pills. He's not taking his pills.

RICHMOND. I will.

LAUREN *leaves* RICHMOND *by the graveside.*

Scene Fifteen

Detention classroom. About five/six weeks later. End of a school day. COCK DAVE *is sat funnily on a chair looking out of a window up into the sky.* RICHMOND *enters, books and newspaper under his arm as usual. Surprised to see* COCK DAVE.

RICHMOND. Hello.

COCK DAVE. Hello.

RICHMOND. Don't see you in here for detention much these days.

COCK DAVE. Aye, it's been a while.

RICHMOND. A whole month I reckon. Ah well, knew it couldn't last. So what've you done?

COCK DAVE. Nought. Just thought I should put in an appearance for me respect's sake.

RICHMOND. Oh.

COCK DAVE. That's all. I am still a Wannabe-Cock, you know.

RICHMOND. You still wanting to be cock of yer year?

COCK DAVE. Oh aye. Aye. Not bothered really. If I can be I will be. I'm not going out of me way to be though. But no one's giving me shit.

RICHMOND. I reckon Palmer will be cock.

COCK DAVE. You're probably right. I'll have a go though. That'll be a detention to look forward to.

RICHMOND. I can't wait.

COCK DAVE. I'll try to get it to co-incide with start of the new season after the summer hols.

RICHMOND. I'm not sure that's a good idea.

COCK DAVE. What you gonna do about it?

RICHMOND. Headmaster's still got you in his sights.

COCK DAVE. I've been behaving. For me.

RICHMOND. Aye for you. But he's still waiting for you to fuck up.

COCK DAVE. Bastard.

RICHMOND. An' I've used up all me powers of persuasion an' brownie points with him after Lauren.

COCK DAVE. Does he blame you for her leaving? But it weren't cos of that.

RICHMOND. I know.

COCK DAVE. Course you did want her to leave, you were encouraging her to.

RICHMOND. Aye.

COCK DAVE. So he's kind of right.

RICHMOND. If you get trouble again, I won't be able to help you.

COCK DAVE. I won't do ought involving teachers, promise. I'll just smack Wannabe-Cocks. That be alright, won't it?

RICHMOND. I wouldn't like to say.

COCK DAVE. Fuck's sake. Well I . . .

RICHMOND. What?

COCK DAVE. Well I don't wanna go to spacker school, do I?

RICHMOND. You don't?

COCK DAVE. No. Have to fucking do nought then, won't I?

RICHMOND. Must admit I thought you'd have been off pursuing yer dream by now.

COCK DAVE. Me dream?

RICHMOND. The room wi' the telly?

COCK DAVE. No.

RICHMOND. At one time you couldn't wait to get there.

COCK DAVE. Yeah well.

RICHMOND. Yeah well what?

COCK DAVE. Nought.

RICHMOND. Well why aren't you there?

COCK DAVE. You want me to be there?

RICHMOND. No.

COCK DAVE. Then what you asking for?

RICHMOND. Just curious.

COCK DAVE. Aye well, you can stay curious.

RICHMOND. Okay. Footie then?

COCK DAVE. Look, I just don't wanna be. I dunno. Just not. Stuff changes, doesn't it?

RICHMOND. No.

COCK DAVE. It does. Her. She wouldn't want me to be there. I'd have to hurt someone to get there. An' if she heard about it, I don't want her to hate me. It's not like I really wanna hurt anyone anyway. Well not all the time I don't. So I haven't. And I won't. Probably.

RICHMOND. Probably.

COCK DAVE. I won't.

RICHMOND. What you looking at?

COCK DAVE. The sky.

RICHMOND. Okay.

COCK DAVE. Well what else is there up there?

RICHMOND. I didn't think that'd be the kind of thing you'd look at.

COCK DAVE. I look at all sorts, me.

RICHMOND. When I look at the sky there always seems to be this greyish tinge to it these days.

COCK DAVE. Yeah?

RICHMOND. I used to think it were the pollution. Then I thought it were just my eyes. Maybe it's a bit of both.

COCK DAVE. You're weird, you.

RICHMOND. Aye.

COCK DAVE. Dunno why I bother with you.

RICHMOND. Neither do I.

COCK DAVE. I don't get so many detentions these days, an' when I do they're normal detentions like.

RICHMOND. Yeah.

COCK DAVE. I miss talking footie wi' you. Specially after summer hols when new season will have started.

RICHMOND. Well you know where I am if you want me.

COCK DAVE. Aye.

RICHMOND. David?

COCK DAVE. Yeah?

RICHMOND. Don't make her hate you.

> COCK DAVE *nods and leaves. For the first time we see* RICHMOND *smile. Opens his paper.*

Scene Sixteen

LAUREN *is sat in the wood, in her new uniform.* COCK DAVE *enters. Sees her. Approaches.*

COCK DAVE. What you doing here? Fuck off. Go away. I don't need you. I'm alright me. I don't want you. No one wants you round here. What you come back for? I'm sick of you in my head, so go. I told you ages ago this is my place for a quiet smoke. You don't come here not ever. You think you can bring yer posh smartarse friends in here for a smoke? Well you fucking can't cos I'll smack 'em. I will. So fuck off out of it bastard face . . . What's wrong?

LAUREN. The kids at the posh smartarse school . . .

COCK DAVE. What about 'em?

LAUREN. They all call me common . . . I dunno what it is, but I just seem to bring the worst out in people.

> *A beat. He sits down next to her, a bit of a space. He lights a fag and holds it out for her. She takes a drag.*

I'm going to have to give these up now.

> *She looks ahead, quiet despair. Unsure, tentatively he puts his hand on her back and rubs it a little – something small and tender.*

End.

A Nick Hern Book

Bottle Universe first published in Great Britain
as a paperback original in 2005 by Nick Hern Books Limited,
14 Larden Road, London W3 7ST in association with
The Bush Theatre, London

Bottle Universe copyright © 2005 Simon Burt

Simon Burt has asserted his right to be identified as
the author of this work

Cover image: Stem Design

Typeset by Country Setting, Kingsdown, Kent CT14 8ES
Printed in Great Britain by Cox and Wyman, Reading, Berks

A CIP catalogue record for this book is available from
the British Library

ISBN-13   978 1 85459 889 9
ISBN-10   1 85459 889 9